COOKING
WILD GAME

COOKING WILD GAME

Zack Hanle

Illustrated by Grambs Miller

Liveright · New York

Liveright
386 Park Avenue South, New York, N.Y. 10016

1.987654321

Cooking wild game.
1. Cookery (Game)   I. Title.
TX751.H36   644.6'9'1   74-11069
ISBN 087140-595-4

To Alan R. Hanle and to
Richard A. and Richard M. Zachariae—
those three musketeers: son,
father and brother—
who filled our tables with epicurean
delights from field, forest, and shore.

In this book you will find both easy-to-cook classics and contemporary ways of preparing game for the table. The recipes are culled from the three-generation collection of a game-hunting, game-eating family on both sides of the Atlantic. During the lean years they ate humble rabbit stew and during the lush, they dined on breast of pheasant in cream. Early on, the children in the family developed a taste for all things wild because of a mother who experimented, tasted, and creatively cooked everything edible that sea, shore, field, and forest offered. As their fortunes grew, so did their tastes for increasingly exotic game flavors, and the men in the family became sportsmen hunters, traveling from Canada and Maine to Florida and Mississippi and out to the Western trails after the big game. The delight in feasting on foods of the chase has been transferred now to a fourth generation of children—and it is hoped that this book will communicate that pleasure to many and perhaps open new vistas of different dining in the home.

The cooking of wild game—or any other food—is a matter of taste. So, too, is the eating of it. And taste varies not only with the individual, but also with the times and with the cultures around the world. Americans, for example, do not generally relish that certain snipe delicacy esteemed by the French because the recipe includes the chopped entrails of the bird. (In fairness, however, not a few gastronomes in our hunting world savor the "trail" of our woodcock roasted right along with the little bird.) Nor do we favor hanging game birds, as in the English tradition, until they are so high in flavor as to be virtually rotten. Yet our Founding Fathers endorsed this practice, and many game fanciers still consider it the only way to bring out inherent wild essences. Oddly enough, spoiled meat is not lethal to the human stomach—as are fish and other foods. But today's palates prefer fresher flesh.

Is taste, then, inherited? Acquired? Or bred of necessity? Both tastes and techniques change with more advanced knowledge of the nature of game and of the culinary arts. Perhaps the greatest change has been wrought with the advent of such modern equipment as the refrigerator, the freezer, and thermostatically controlled cooking, baking, broiling, and roasting. It is many moons since those pioneer days when the homemaker's kitchen and cool room were festooned with furred and feathered game, and preparing dinner was more than one day's job. After aging · and eviscerating, there was skinning, plucking, marinating, and finally either hours of stewing, casseroling, or spit-roasting the spoils for the hungry hordes at her table. But those are ghosts of repasts past. Today, a few days in the refrigerator "cures" the fresh-killed bird, a friendly butcher cuts the venison in ready-to-cook roasts, chops, and stew meat, and wraps them for your freezer, and recipes for cooking are incredibly simplified with the assist of convenience ingredients. And for those who do not enjoy the hunt, there is game galore in the marketplace, at prices comparable to those for prime beef and milk-fed veal. (A better buy, actually, since game is higher in protein, lower in cholesterol-producing fat.)

The aim of this book has been to make these dishes practical as well as palatable, simple as well as savory, and workable as well as rewarding in the eating. (Joseph Conrad once said: "The intention of every other piece of prose may be discussed and even mistrusted; but the purpose of a cookery book is one and unmistakable. Its object can conceivably be no other than to increase the happiness of mankind.")

The recipes and instructions are a matter of personal taste, but expanded to incorporate as much variation as possible. There will be debatable points; there always are in any cookbook. The hunter who has feasted at the campsite, the gastronome at his food-and-wine-club dinner, the knowledgeable cook at home—all will have heated discussions, some of which have continued since Neanderthal tossed the first haunch into his newfound glowing toy. How long should you cook a mallard? Blood rare, you say?

Madness. How hot should the oven be? Very? Sacrilege; the bird will be crisped to a cinder. How big is a partridge? Three bites, says the North Carolinian. A meal, says the Down Easter. Skin the bird? Never. But, of course. Wash it? Horrors. Lard it? No, bard it. No, neither of these.

But do not discuss for long. The bird waits. The recipes are here. You may wish to revise the sizes of portions if you have a houseful of gourmandizers who have been out jogging at something all day. You may choose to sear the meat in your own special way, or add a favorite ingredient of your own. You alone know the tastes of your feeders and their capacity for consumption. No recipe in this book—nor in any other book—is an ultimate. Each is and should be a guide, and all who read here are exhorted to modify, substitute, change, and expand at will and to vary to taste. The object is: be more creative and enjoy the doing as well as the feasting.

Ship Bottom, New Jersey   ZACK HANLE
April 1974

Whether you buy or bag your wild game, it demands special care and handling if it is to appear on the dining table as the epicurean delight it is and should be. If you're lucky, you have a hunter in your home—or a friend who gifts you with trophies of the chase. You are even luckier if the hunter knows how to insure that his prize is properly dressed for the cook so that the prepared bird or beast will be of superior flavor and texture. Lacking a provider, however, you need not be deprived of the pleasures of serving game in your home. Throughout the country there are fine butcher shops, specialty meat markets, and an increasing number of gourmet supermarkets offering quail, pheasant, venison, duck, goose, rabbit, hare, turkey, venison, and other big and small game. (Turn to pages 211–212 for a list of just a few of these.) Most of the game sold is raised in natural-habitat conditions on specially licensed game farms and preserves. Some game is imported for raising on game preserves and some reaches the shops and marketplaces when the government grazing grounds or private ranches thin certain herds. Both the sale of game commercially and the amounts of game taken by hunters is strictly regulated by law.

The sportsman afield may learn how to take care of fresh-killed game by studying any good hunter's handbook as well as the magazines devoted to hunting. And how the wild bird or beast is handled is extremely important. Since this book's chief concern is with the preparation of ready-to-cook game, the following is the briefest synopsis of what should happen to game before it reaches the kitchen:

For *large game* (deer, elk, et al.) the basics are: bleed, draw, clean, and cool immediately on site. Spread the cavity with a stick and hang by hind legs or antlers until cooled. Avoid heat in transport. Hang, or age, in a cool place or outdoors if temperatures are between 36 and 40 degrees Fahrenheit. Allow a full week for the meat of young animals to firm; two to three weeks for older ones. If the hide has not been removed before, do so just before butchering the meat. The carcass should be butchered in the same way as beef cuts, and most of the fat should be removed and discarded. Refrigerate and cook as needed, keeping the meat refrigerated no longer than beef can be refrigerated. Wrap what is not to be used and freeze (freezing timetable and instructions, page 142).

For *small game* (hare, rabbit, squirrel, et al.): skin, draw, clean, and cool at once (with the exception of animals like opossum which are not skinned as will be noted later). Carefully remove, without piercing, the scent glands under forelegs and near spine at lower back. Avoid heat in transport. Refrigerate one or two days before cooking or freezing.

For *game birds* (geese, ducks, quail, et al.): pluck, draw, clean, and cool at once. (Exceptions are birds which, according to individual taste, are to be hung for a while.) Remove oil sac at tail base and, in the case of a sage- or spruce-feeding bird, remove craw immediately. Keep bird's skin intact while plucking; the easiest way is to do this while the bird is still warm, pulling feathers in the direction of growth. Down feathers may be singed carefully and pinfeathers may be removed with fingers or tweezers. The hunter may be too occupied in the field to pluck birds at once, but evisceration should take place promptly. Later they may be plucked by dipping them in melted paraffin, letting the paraffin cool and pulling feathers and paraffin off all at once. Avoid heat in transporting birds and cool them faster by hanging them from a belt or strap in the open air rather than stuffing them into game pockets. Refrigerate birds for 2–3 days before cooking or freezing.

Purchasing game from a market or butcher usually assures you of meat that has been properly aged and handled when the animal or bird was killed. It should also assure you of having tender meat of good flavor. Hence, long marinating is not necessary. However, you may be presented with, say, a piece of venison of unknown or advanced age and considerable toughness. A nonseasoned meat tenderizer used according to package directions is the short route, but not the epicure's way. Long, slow cooking—as in braising or stewing—or so-called "moist cooking" is another way. But the most effective method is to marinate. (Turn to page 149 for details and marinade recipes.) Often the cut of meat or bird may then be treated to a wide variety of cooking techniques after this corrective procedure.

Veteran hunters as well as experienced chefs and game cooks know all the tricks, shortcuts, and special tips that make for superior wild game dishes. Following are 58 miscellaneous pointers gathered from these sources:

1. Venison fat, because it is so strongly flavored (and sometimes because it becomes rancid from exposure to air) should be trimmed completely from the meat—both before cooking and before freezing. The same is true of other big game, especially bear, unless the animal is very young and freshly killed (young bear grease, rendered, is highly prized as a cooking fat by many game cooks). These animals should never be cooked with or in their own fat. Larding (page 200) or covering roasts with fat salt pork (barding) is recommended for roasts, and basting with butter, margarine, or bacon drippings is best for chops, cutlets, or steaks.

2. Venison liver and heart are both excellent variety meats and may be prepared as the liver and heart of beef are.

3. Freshly butchered venison should be washed quickly

and carefully with cold water. Inspect it for hair from the hide sticking to the meat. Then thoroughly wipe the flesh dry before cooking.

4. Bear, boar, and the collared peccary—like pork—are possible trichinosis carriers and therefore should be cooked thoroughly to at least 150° F. internal temperature.

5. Salvage venison and other big game cuts which are too high or over-gamey from poor handling in the field (but still edible) by marinating them overnight in a half-and-half mixture of beer and vinegar with a handful of salt. Then drain and boil in salt water for 20 minutes. Drain again and use only for stewing. This works well for moose, reindeer, antelope, elk, caribou, and bear.

6. Rabbit and hare should be hung head down. When skinned and dressed, the hare will be found to have blood collected under the ribs. This should be saved to add to accompanying gravies, sauces, and stews.

7. Woodchuck or groundhog must have all excess fat removed as well as the kernel-like glands beneath the front legs and along the spine (7–9 kernels in all, depending on the age of the animal) which give the animal an unappetizing flavor and aroma.

8. The best opossum is a fat one (taken in freezing weather), but its fat should be boiled off. Parboil the meat in salt water for about 1 hour and pour off and skim the fat continually. Finally, drain entirely before roasting. *Note:* In dressing opossum, do not overlook the glands beneath the front legs and at the small of the back; if not removed, the animal will be unappetizing. Do not skin, but dip in scalding water and pull out the hairs, then wash and scrub the skin.

9. Rabbit purchased from the butcher is, of course, free of disease. (It is inspected by the USDA.) But the hunter should inspect this game animal carefully, despite the fact that most rabbits are not carrying tularemia. Use rubber gloves when dressing rabbit, and, after cleaning it, wash hands thoroughly with hot, soapy water. Thorough cooking will kill bacteria, but freezing will not. A rabbit with suspected tularemia should be discarded. Tularemia is evidenced in the form of small white growths in the liver of the rabbit and is transferred through the skin of human beings.

10. Raccoon is good only when caught in cold, freezing weather. To prepare it for roasting, remove all fat and the scent glands along either side of the backbone and in the small of the back, as well as under each front leg. Soak it in cold water for at least 3 hours, drain and parboil in water for 1 hour.

11. Furred game does not require too much seasoning, except in some special recipes; go easy with the pepper, cayenne, and spices.

12. Serve all game piping hot on heated serving platters and plates. A big game steak will benefit by being placed on a hot platter (kept hot over boiling water, if necessary) with a lump of butter swirled on the platter.

13. Determine the age of game first in order to cook it or prepare it for cooking correctly. Old game requires longer hanging or aging and subsequent marinating. It most often is best braised, stewed, or otherwise treated to long, slow cooking. A young hare or rabbit has soft paws and ears; old ones have worn paws, stiff and rough ears. Old geese have few pinfeathers, very large wing spurs and red bills; young, tender, moist geese have some down on the legs and the undersides of the bills are soft, not leathery. A baby or yearling pheasant is distinguished from an old bird by its pliable upper beak and its pointed rather than rounded first wing feather tip. Young grouse may be recognized by their clean claws and soft breastbone tips; there is no molting ridge on the legs of the young bird. The age of big game is generally determined by size (see average sizes, pages 139–140) and, of course, the younger the animal, the tenderer the meat.

14. As a general rule, conserve the precious juices of venison and similar big game steaks, chops, and cutlets by salting *after* broiling, rarely before or during the cooking process.

15. Never wash a duck or any other game bird when it is being eviscerated. Duck blood ideally, and if convenient, should be saved and used in gravies or sauces accompanying it.

16. When collecting duck blood for cooking, add a little lemon juice, vinegar, or wine to it to prevent it from coagulating.

17. The oil sac in the tail of the duck should be removed immediately after the bird is killed. It has a particularly unpleasant flavor which, left for any length of time, can permeate the entire bird.

18. Soak excessively fishy-flavored marine birds in salt or vinegar water overnight to get rid of the objectionable flavor. While water-soaking birds is not usually advisable, in these cases the procedure could make an otherwise unpalatable bird edible.

19. The European practice of hanging game birds for long periods of time to improve flavor is not widely practiced in the United States. The birds purchased in the

market are properly aged and need no further hanging. Sportsmen in the field, however, often find it practical to hang birds for 24–48 hours in the cool, open air. If the weather is very cold, up to a week is acceptable. If the temperature is too high, the risk of spoilage is great.

20. If you're bent on hanging your hunter's pheasant, then 4 days to a week is the rule, weather permitting. (Europeans often say that the bird is ready to cook when the longest tail feather can be easily plucked.) Feathers should be left on, since some of the oil in them imparts a better flavor to the flesh.

21. If a dramatic presentation of roast pheasant at the table is desired, have the hunter or the butcher reserve the entire head, wing tips, and tail feathers of the cock pheasant. Serve the pheasant on a silver tray and place the head, wings, and tail appropriately. The dish is spectacular and the same "garnishing" with feathers may be done with a cold bird.

22. Cook white meat birds, such as pheasant, until juices run golden and clear. Cook most dark meat birds, especially ducks, rare.

23. Save duck, goose, and small bird livers for making pâtés, giblet gravies, stuffings and dressings, soups, stocks, and stews. In fact, save all the giblets from most birds for these purposes.

24. A quail should be eaten, ideally, the day after it is killed or as soon thereafter as possible. It should be plucked and singed immediately after killing, and should be drawn from the neck end after head and neck have been removed.

25. Handle pigeons and doves with great care in order not to damage the delicate skin. When purchasing these birds, choose plump, large ones with light-colored flesh.

26. For an interesting flavor, stuff partridge and quail with vine leaves (grape) when roasting them.

27. If you've acquired a too-gamey wild goose, don't stuff it; it is often bitter tasting and permeates the stuffing or dressing as well. Better to fill the cavity with quartered raw potatoes and discard them before serving the goose.

28. Even the smallest birds, stuffed or not, should have their cavities closed before roasting in order to keep them moist and tender.

29. If a greenish tinge appears on the thin skin of a duck's abdomen, this does not indicate decay or that the bird is inedible. The color commonly appears after the bird has hung for 2 or 3 days.

30. Use dry paper towels or a clean cloth to wipe out birds. If they are to be sprinkled with lemon juice or spirits, soak a small piece of cloth in the liquid and wipe the bird with this to get even distribution of moisture.

31. When mincing or slicing small livers and other giblets as well as pieces of meat, work with very cold meat rather than limp, room-temperature flesh for easier and quicker handling.

32. Excessively fishy-flavored marine and shorebirds can be improved by being skinned. These include brant, coot, and other members of the duck family, but skinning is not always necessary. The coot in particular can be too strong in flavor for the average taste, and skinning it also removes its fatty layer which is permeated with most of that flavor.

33. When making gravies and sauces for big game that call for spirits in the ingredients, bear in mind that port, Madeira, sherry, and claret may be interchanged without appreciably affecting the results.

34. When preparing dressings and stuffings, generally allow 1 cup for each 1 pound of bird.

35. Oven roasting bags are excellent for cooking exceptionally dry game, since only minimal moisture is lost.

36. Wild goose acquired by the sportsman tends to be lean and, if young, it should be cooked like duck, but well done rather than rare as in the case of the latter. Pen-raised birds are fatty and the fat is strong; these should not, as stated, usually be stuffed nor should the fat be used for gravies or sauces.

37. Too strong-flavored birds may be "deodorized" by stuffing them with parsley, raw apple, celery, onion, or potato (or a combination of these), all of which absorb odors. Then discard the bird contents before serving.

38. Always cool dressing before stuffing any bird, and remove all dressing from large birds when storing leftovers in the refrigerator. Never freeze a bird with stuffing in it.

39. Always remove meat from its marinade and drain it an hour or two before cooking time.

40. Sinews, nerves, and second skin should be removed from all big game before cooking.

41. The hanging of game does not tenderize it; it is done to enhance the "wild" flavor. Certain marinades do the tenderizing (page 149).

42. For those who object to spirits as ingredients in the preparation of game, it should be understood that only the essential *flavor* of wines and brandies and beer remains after cooking. The alcoholic content is burned off in the

process. Spirits are used to enhance as well as to keep the meat moist. In many cases, cider may be comfortably substituted for white wine and beef or game stock for red wine. There is no nonalcoholic substitute for cognac and brandy.

43. Freezing neither improves nor tenderizes game or any other meat. It simply maintains the status quo. If not properly frozen, game will lose moisture and become drier, hence tougher and often stringy.

44. While freezing ground meat is thoroughly acceptable, remember that game meat lacks fat and loses moisture more rapidly. Either freeze meat to be ground in pieces and grind it when thawed and ready to cook or grind the game meat with some fat—about ¼ pound of fat to ¾ pound of meat—before freezing.

45. Allow 2 cups of gravy for a 6-pound roast or bird— or more, as desired.

46. If a sauce or gravy is too thick, thin it with more of one of the major liquid ingredients rather than with water.

47. If gravy is too thin, continue stirring over heat until it is the desired consistency, or add a little more flour which has been blended with one of the liquid ingredients.

48. If game is dusted with or rolled in flour for the pur-

pose of browning it, less flour will be necessary in making any gravy accompanying it.

49. Save and use leftover wines and fruit juice for making marinades and sauces.

50. In general, when a recipe calls for fresh herbs and none is available, use half as much dried equivalent as the amount specified in the recipe.

51. Wild game has its own special flavor which should not be masked by overpowering sauces or too much gravy. If a piece of game or bird is too "high" and powerful in flavor for your taste, marinate it longer.

52. Most game birds are by nature very dry (except pen-fed wild geese) and therefore must be kept moist and succulent by the addition of or basting with fat, oil, butter, or margarine.

53. Whenever possible prepare stock from the game being cooked and use it when called for in a recipe. If this is not possible, use a compatible stock or broth, such as chicken broth or stock for pheasant, partridge, quail, etc., and beef stock or bouillon for moose, venison, elk, etc.

54. Whether to wash a bird or simply to wipe it out is controversial. If wild game birds are brought to the kitchen with excessive blood clots and pieces of viscera clinging to

the interior, it may be necessary to wash the cavities with water.

55. Rubbing any bird inside and out with a cut lemon improves flavor and is a fine compromise in the debate of whether to wash or not.

56. Try half oil and half butter or margarine for a faster, crispier browning of meats and birds.

57. Lacking time or ingredients for marinating a bird or game cut, try smearing it with yogurt and let stand for an hour or more at room temperature; then wipe off.

58. Above all, do not serve wild game to guests who do not appreciate it and would prefer a beefsteak or a roast chicken to, say, venison or pheasant.

The term "venison" once applied to the meat of any animal of the hunt. Today it generally refers only to the meat of antlered animals—deer, elk, antelope, reindeer, moose—and most specifically to deer meat. Most of the venison in the markets is deer meat, although elk appears in very special shops, and reindeer meat, usually smoked, is occasionally available as an import. Venison in the market is usually raised on preserves and the chops, steaks, and cutlets from young deer are most prized. These may be cooked as the comparable cuts of beef. The rump, breast, neck, round, and shoulder are best braised or stewed or ground. The haunch, rack, saddle, baron, leg, and loin are superb when roasted. Recipes for venison may be used for all the antlered family. Since the flesh of these animals is rather dry, it requires larding or barding (generous wrappings of fat salt pork). Meat from older animals is tougher and improves with marinating. If wild venison has an "off" flavor or gamey taste, it probably has not been properly handled in the dressing out and hanging. Venison purchased in fine specialty meat markets, however, should have no tainted or over-gamey flavor, nor should it be stringy or tough.

Buffalo or bison is available from time to time in specialty shops when the government prunes the herds. Bear appears in markets, and sometimes may be ordered when sufficient advance notice is given. It is a fatty meat and should be cooked like domestic pork, although it has more the flavor and texture of beef. So, too, should wild boar and the collared peccary be cooked and, unless the animal is very young, it should be treated to a Fatty Game Marinade (page 152). The chops and ribs of these animals are excellent with sauerkraut, but long, slow cooking is important —just as for domestic pork—in order to destroy any possible trichinae.

Mountain goat or any other wild goat, if young and tender, may be cooked like suckling pig or domestic lamb. Older, tougher cuts of these animals should be stewed for several hours. Like boar, the young mountain goat is exceedingly succulent and flavorsome when spit- or oven-roasted whole.

Dall and desert sheep should be treated and cooked like venison, and the recipes that serve for venison work well for this game.

Roast Loin of Venison

1 tender loin of venison (3–4 pounds)
  Fat salt pork strips for larding (page 200)
  Salt, pepper
2 small onions stuck with 1 clove each
1 cup orange juice
½ cup melted butter or margarine
1 teaspoon crushed dried rosemary
½ cup tart currant or Wild Beach Plum Jelly (page 184)
1 tablespoon grated lemon peel
1 tablespoon instant flour

Lard the loin with the salt pork strips and season all over with salt, pepper. Place in preheated oven at 450° F. for 15 minutes to sear and seal in juices. Add onions, orange juice, melted butter, and rosemary. Cover with lid of roasting pan. Lower heat to 325° and roast for 15 minutes per pound. Baste frequently with pan liquids. Meanwhile melt the jelly and add the lemon peel. About 10 minutes before meat is done, brush all surfaces with the melted jelly mixture. Transfer to heated platter and keep warm. Skim pan liquids of excess fat. Strain 2 cups of remaining liquids and heat in saucepan. Sprinkle flour in and heat, stirring, till thickened. Serve as gravy. Serves 4–6.
Serve with: wild rice and raw spinach salad.

Venison Chops with Chestnuts

6 venison chops, ¾ inch thick
  Salt, pepper
2 tablespoons butter or margarine
1½ cups Chestnut Purée (page 173)
3 tablespoons red currant jelly
½ cup canned tomato sauce or ½ cup chili sauce
  Fresh mint sprigs

Sprinkle chops with salt, pepper. Melt butter in skillet large enough to hold chops snugly side by side. Cook for 5 minutes on each side. Arrange the chestnut purée in a mound in center of a heated platter. Arrange chops around this. Pour off all but 2 tablespoons of pan drippings. Add jelly and stir until melted. Add tomato sauce, mix, and heat through, stirring. Pour over chops. Garnish with fresh mint springs. Serves 6.
Serve with: Braised Celery (page 179).

Venison Sauerbraten

3½ pounds venison stewing meat in 1 piece
2 teaspoons salt
½ teaspoon pepper
2 medium onions, sliced
1 medium carrot, sliced
1 large stalk celery, sliced (top included)
4 whole cloves
4 crushed peppercorns
2 bay leaves, crumbled
2 cups vinegar
½ stick butter or margarine
12 small gingersnaps, crushed with rolling pin
1 tablespoon sugar
2 tablespoons flour mixed with ¼ cup water

Season meat with salt, pepper. Place in crock, ceramic or glass bowl and add onions, carrot, celery, cloves, peppercorns, bay leaves, and vinegar. Cover and refrigerate for 3 days, turning several times a day in the marinade. Drain; reserve marinade. Wipe meat dry. Melt butter in deep pan or Dutch oven and brown meat on all sides. Add strained marinade and bring to boil. Lower heat and simmer, covered, for 2–3 hours or until meat is cooked through and tender. Transfer meat to heated platter and keep warm.

Bring pan juices to boil and add gingersnaps and sugar. Stir over medium heat until thickened. If necessary to thicken further, add flour-water mixture and continue cooking to desired thickness. Pour sauce over meat. Serves 6.
Serve with: Parsley Potato Dumplings (page 174) and Bavarian Cabbage (page 180).
Note: Buffalo, elk, moose may be substituted for deer.

Rack of Venison

1 rack of young deer (about 6–7 ribs)
¼ pound chilled fat salt pork larding strips
4 peppercorns, crushed
4 juniper berries, crushed
2 teaspoons salt
1 stick butter or margarine, melted
1 pint sour cream, heated
2 tablespoons potato flour
1 cup beef stock or strong bouillon
2 tablespoons tart red currant jelly

Lard the meat at 2-inch intervals in 2 rows. Place in roasting pan and sprinkle with peppercorns, juniper berries, and salt. Pour melted butter over meat and roast in preheated 400° F. oven for 15 minutes; then lower heat to 375° and continue roasting until meat thermometer registers "rare" for beef. Baste every 15 minutes with pan juices and, when meat begins to brown, add the heated sour cream to the pan. Transfer meat to heated platter and keep warm. Skim excess fat from pan juices and strain juices into saucepan. Stir in flour and blend over medium heat until thickened. Add stock to make 1½ cups; cook to desired thickness. Add jelly and stir; serve on side. Serves 6.
Serve with: wild rice and Bavarian Cabbage (page 180).

Venison Fillets

2 venison fillets cut from saddle (about 6 pounds)
¼ pound fat salt pork cut in larding strips
¼ pound lean ham cut in larding strips
1½ cups Venison Marinade (page 155)
6 slices bacon
1 large onion, sliced thin
1 cup dry red wine
2 tablespoons butter or margarine
2 tablespoons flour
1 cup beef stock or bouillon, heated
½ cup Madeira or port, heated
¼ cup sour cream, warmed
1 tablespoon shredded orange peel
1 tablespoon shredded lemon peel

Lard the fillets with alternate strips of fat and ham at 2-inch intervals. Cover with the marinade and refrigerate, covered, for 8 hours or overnight. Drain (reserve marinade) and dry with paper towels. Line bottom of roasting pan with bacon and the onion slices. Place meat on top and pour wine and 1 cup of strained marinade into pan. Roast in preheated 350° F. oven for 50 minutes or until meat thermometer registers "rare" for beef. Cook longer as desired, but do not overcook or meat will be tough and dry. Transfer fillets to heated platter and keep warm. Reserve pan juices. Meanwhile, melt butter in skillet and blend in the flour till smooth. Slowly stir in the heated stock and Madeira and simmer, stirring, until sauce thickens. Strain pan juices and remaining marinade and add to the sauce with all remaining ingredients. Simmer till slightly thickened. Serve on side with the sliced fillets. Serves 10–12.

Serve with: wild rice and Braised Escarole Amandine (page 182).

Note: Recipe also works for caribou, antelope, elk fillets.

Venison in Chestnut Cream

2 *pounds venison slices cut from loin, each* ½ *inch thick*
6 *tablespoons butter*
1½ *cups semisweet white wine, warmed*
1 *cup heavy cream, warmed*
1 *tablespoon minced fresh parsley*
½ *cup Chestnut Purée (page 173)*
   Salt, pepper

Pound venison slices to ¼-inch thickness (or have butcher do this as for veal scallopini). Stack 3 or 4 slices and with a sharp knife cut into 1½ x ½-inch strips. Melt butter in a heavy skillet and toss the meat strips in this, stirring over low heat until almost all of the butter has been absorbed. Stir in the wine. Add cream and turn up heat to medium. Bring mixture to a boil, but do not boil. Stir in chestnut purée and lower heat. Simmer, stirring until slightly thickened. Serves 4–6.

Serve with: hot toast points spread with pâté de foie gras or Goose Liver Pâté (page 128) and place under the broiler for 2–3 minutes. Garnish with watercress.

Venison Pie

2 pounds boneless venison, cut in 1-inch cubes

Flour

Salt, pepper

1 stick butter or margarine

2 cups beef stock or bouillon

1 cup red wine

1 bay leaf

½ teaspoon crushed dried rosemary

2 tablespoons finely chopped fresh parsley

24 button mushrooms

12 small whole white onions

2 packages of frozen peas, thawed

3 cups fluffy whipped potatoes

1 egg yolk, lightly beaten

1 tablespoon water

Dredge venison in flour and sprinkle with salt, pepper. Melt butter in heatproof casserole and quickly brown meat evenly. Add stock or bouillon and the wine; turn up heat for 2–3 minutes till liquid boils. Lower heat and add bay leaf, rosemary, and fresh parsley. Cover and simmer gently for 1½ hours. Add mushrooms and onions. Cook till onions are tender. Add peas. Cook till peas are just tender but still crisp. Remove from heat. Stir in 2 tablespoons of the whipped potatoes. Cover top of meat-vegetable mixture with thick layer of the potatoes. Swirl top and brush lightly with the egg yolk thinned with the tablespoon of water. Place in 400° F. oven until potatoes are golden brown. Serves 4–6.

Serve with: mixed green salad.

Note: Instead of the potatoes, pie may be topped with a pastry crust (bake at 450° F. till golden) or with old-fashioned dumplings placed close together and sprinkled with finely chopped fresh parsley.

Venison Chops in Foil

8 tender venison chops, ½ inch thick
1 stick butter or margarine
2 small onions, chopped fine
8 medium mushrooms, sliced
2 tablespoons minced fresh parsley
¼ teaspoon salt
¼ teaspoon freshly ground black pepper
  Heavy-duty aluminum foil
8 thin slices cold boiled ham
8 tablespoons sour cream

Melt ½ butter in large heavy skillet and sauté the chops for 10 minutes. Transfer to a heated plate and keep warm. Melt remaining butter in skillet and sauté onions, mushrooms, and parsley until golden. Sprinkle with salt, pepper. Turn off heat and prepare foil packets. Cut 8 pieces of foil, each about 12 x 14 inches. On each piece, place in center 1 piece of the ham. Top with a venison chop. Add a generous tablespoon or more of the mushroom-onion-parsley mixture. Add 1 tablespoon sour cream and seal securely. Place in preheated 350° F. oven for 20 minutes. Serve in foil or arrange packet contents on platter. Serves 4.
Serve with: Baked Stuffed Mushrooms (page 182).

Roast Saddle of Venison

1 saddle of young deer (5–6 pounds), trimmed, all sinews
  removed
½ pound fat salt pork, cut in larding strips, chilled
  Salt, pepper
½ cup melted butter or margarine
1 tablespoon lemon juice
1 cup Basic White Sauce (page 157), warmed

Lard the saddle with the chilled pork strips, place in roasting pan, and brush with melted butter. Sprinkle all over with salt, pepper. Roast in preheated 425° F. oven for 40–50 minutes for rare, longer for medium or well done. Brush with additional butter every 10 minutes. Remove to heated platter and keep warm. Skim excess fat from roasting pan, place over medium heat, and stir in the lemon juice. Add the warmed white sauce, stir till heated through, and serve in sauceboat with the meat. Serves 4–6.
Serve with: Brussels Sprouts with Grapes (page 178) and wild or brown rice.

Venison Chops with Gin

8 small venison chops or cutlets
2 tablespoons butter or margarine
3 tablespoons genever or Dutch gin, warmed
2 crushed juniper berries
  Pinch basil
¼ cup Basic Brown Sauce (page 157), heated
½ cup heavy cream, warmed
  Juice of ¼ lemon

Brown chops in melted butter in large skillet, turning once and cooking for about 4–5 minutes on each side. Transfer chops to heated platter. Add gin to skillet and ignite. When flames die, stir and scrape pan to get all of the essences. Add the juniper berries, basil, and brown sauce, stirring over low heat. Slowly add the cream, blend, and heat through. Sprinkle with lemon juice and pour over chops. Serves 4.

Serve with: crisp buttered toast triangles and Prune-Raisin Relish (page 185).

Herbed Venison Cutlet

2 venison cutlets (from leg or loin), 1½ inches thick
8 fat salt pork strips for larding, chilled
1 cup vegetable oil
2 tablespoons fresh chopped parsley
1 tablespoon minced chives
1 large shallot, minced fine
6 slices bacon
1 tablespoon flour mixed with 2 tablespoons water
1 cup beef stock, bouillon, or consommé
1 teaspoon lemon juice or wine vinegar
  Salt, pepper

Lard the cutlets at 3-inch intervals with salt pork strips. Combine oil, parsley, chives, and shallot, and marinate cutlets in this mixture for 3–4 hours. Drain; reserve marinade. Place cutlets in a shallow roasting pan, cover with bacon slices, and pour in marinade. Roast in preheated 325° oven for about 45 minutes or until tender, but still pink when fork-tested. Transfer cutlets to heated platter and keep warm. Skim fat from pan and bring drippings to boil over medium-high heat. Stir in flour mixture and add stock, stirring over high heat until slightly thickened. Add lemon juice and season to taste. Pour over cutlets. Serves 4–6.

Serve with: creamed spinach or Chestnut Purée (page 173).

Baron of Venison

1 baron (sirloin and leg section) of venison, about 6 pounds
  Red Wine Marinade (page 153)
  Salt
  Freshly ground black pepper
  Sauce Poivrade (page 158)

Place venison in a deep nonmetallic container and pour in marinade. Set in a cool place for at least 48 hours, turning meat several times a day so that marinade permeates all surfaces. Drain; reserve marinade. Pour marinade into deep roasting pan. Season meat with salt and pepper and place in pan. Roast in preheated 300° F. oven for 1½ hours, then at 450° for 15 minutes more. (A meat thermometer should read "medium" for veal when venison is done.) Transfer to heated platter and serve at once with sauce poivrade on side. Serves 4–6.
Serve with: Braised Endive (page 179).

Curry of Venison

2 pounds boned shoulder of venison, cut in 1-inch cubes
2 tablespoons vegetable oil
5 tablespoons butter or margarine
2 cloves garlic, minced
3 large onions, sliced thin
2 level tablespoons good curry powder (or more, to taste)
2 large stalks celery, sliced in ¼-inch rounds
2½ cups chicken stock, broth, or bouillon
1 tablespoon cornstarch mixed with 2 tablespoons water
½ teaspoon salt
½ cup raisins

Heat oil in a large skillet and brown the meat. In another skillet or Dutch oven, melt butter and stir in garlic, onions, curry powder, and celery. Cook over medium heat, stirring occasionally, until vegetables are soft (about 4 minutes). Add meat and stock. Cover and simmer until meat is tender (about 1–1½ hours). Stir in cornstarch mixture and salt; add raisins. Bring to boil, stirring, and lower heat; simmer 15 minutes more. Serves 4–6.
Serve with: chutney and fluffy white rice.

Roast Leg of Venison

1 leg of venison (about 6 pounds)
  Red Wine Marinade (page 153), cooled
12 larding strips, chilled
 1 stick butter or margarine
 1 tablespoon powdered ginger
 1 tablespoon cornstarch dissolved in 2 tablespoons water
  Salt, pepper

Pour marinade over meat in a large ceramic or porcelain-lined container. Cover; refrigerate for at least 24 hours, turning meat often so that marinade will permeate all surfaces. Drain, reserving the marinade. Wipe meat dry. With a larding needle, insert 2-inch pieces of the larding strips all over at 2- to 3-inch intervals. Place meat in roasting pan and rub all surfaces with butter. Sprinkle with ginger and pour the marinade around the meat. Roast in a preheated 350° F. oven for 2 hours or until meat thermometer registers 150°. (Meat should be pink but not blood rare.) Transfer to a heated platter and keep warm while preparing gravy. Strain marinade and pan juices into a saucepan. Stir in the cornstarch mixture. Bring to boil, stirring, but do not boil. When slightly thickened, add salt and pepper to taste. Serve with the roast. Serves 8.
Serve with: Bavarian Cabbage (page 180).

Spitted Haunch of Venison

1 boned haunch or leg of venison (about 6–7 pounds)
2 cups Red Wine Marinade (page 153)
2 cloves garlic, split
5 strips salt pork to cover entire haunch

Marinate venison in refrigerator or cool room for at least 24 hours (up to 72 hours), turning now and then so that all surfaces are exposed to the marinade. Drain, reserving marinade, and wipe dry. Rub with the split pieces of garlic. With butcher's cord, tie salt pork strips around meat. Center and balance on revolving spit and roast for 1½–2 hours, basting every 15 minutes with the reserved marinade. Remove string and pork strips. Serves 8.
Serve with: Wine Sauce (page 160) and hot Whole Fresh Cranberry (page 183) or lingonberry sauce.

Venison Goulash

3 pounds venison shoulder, breast, or leg, cut in 1½-inch
  cubes
¼ cup flour
1 cup finely chopped onion
½ stick butter or margarine
1 tablespoon paprika
1 teaspoon salt
¼ teaspoon black pepper
1 cup water
1 tablespoon tomato paste
1 green pepper, seeded, diced
1½ cups sour cream, warmed

Coat meat with flour and set aside. In a Dutch oven or heatproof casserole with tight lid, melt butter and sauté onions until golden. Add meat and brown over medium heat. Add paprika, salt, and pepper. Stir in 3 tablespoons water, the tomato paste, and green pepper. Cover, lower heat, and simmer until meat is tender, adding additional water from time to time to prevent sticking. (About 2 hours is required for young, tender venison; longer, for older, tougher meat.) Add sour cream and heat, stirring over low heat for 2–3 minutes more. Serves 6.
Serve with: Parsley Potato Dumplings (page 174).

Venison Pot Roast

2 pounds boned and rolled shoulder of venison
1 tablespoon flour
½ teaspoon salt
½ teaspoon freshly ground black pepper
1 teaspoon powdered ginger
1 tablespoon sugar
½ stick butter or margarine
8 whole peppercorns
½ teaspoon powdered allspice
1 tablespoon grated lemon peel
1 cup beef stock, bouillon, or consommé
1 cup water
½ cup port or Madeira wine
2 teaspoons flour mixed with 2 tablespoons water
½ cup heavy cream, warmed

Wipe and dry meat. Mix together flour, salt, pepper, ginger, and sugar; coat all surfaces of meat with mixture. Melt butter in Dutch oven and brown meat. Add remaining ingredients except flour paste and cream. Cover and simmer for 2 hours or until tender. Strain pot juices; keep roast warm. Heat juice and stir in flour paste until thickened. Stir in cream. Bring to boil. Serve on side. Serves 4.
Serve with: peas and Rosemary Onions (page 176).

Salmi of Venison

2 cups cooked roast venison, cut in bite-size cubes
3 tablespoons butter or margarine
3 tablespoons flour
2 cups hot beef stock or bouillon
  Dash Worcestershire sauce
¼ teaspoon salt
  Pinch pepper
3 tablespoons sherry, port, claret, or red wine
2 cups mushrooms, sliced, sautéed in butter
1 teaspoon minced fresh parsley
4 slices toast, trimmed, quartered for toast points
  Watercress or parsley for garnish

Melt butter in heavy skillet and blend in flour. While stirring, slowly add stock, Worcestershire, salt, pepper, wine. Continue stirring over medium heat until thickened. Lower heat; add meat, mushrooms, and parsley. Heat through; serve with toast points and garnish. Serves 4.
Serve with: chutney or a sweet-sour relish.
Note: Cooked elk or reindeer may be substituted for the venison.

Venison Stew

3 pounds venison shoulder cut in 2-inch cubes
4 tablespoons flour
1 stick butter or margarine
¾ teaspoon salt
2 cups hot beef bouillon
4 cups hot water
1 medium onion, peeled, stuck with 3 cloves
5 peppercorns
1 bay leaf
½ teaspoon crushed dried rosemary
¼ teaspoon thyme
½ teaspoon grated lemon peel
½ cup red wine

Roll meat in flour. In a deep, heavy kettle melt butter and brown the meat. Sprinkle with salt and add bouillon and water. Add all remaining ingredients except wine, stir, and bring to boil. Lower heat, cover and simmer for 1–1½ hours or until meat is tender. Add wine and continue simmering for 15 minutes. Serves 4–6.
Serve with: Parsley Potato Dumplings (page 174).

Broiled Venison Steak

1 loin of venison steak (1–2 pounds) ¾ inch thick
2 tablespoons melted butter or margarine
  Salt, pepper

Trim away any fat from the steak. Preheat broiler and coat top of steak with half the butter. Broil for about 4 minutes, turn, coat with remaining butter, and broil for 3 minutes more. Season lightly with salt, pepper. Serves 2 or more, depending on size of steak.
Serve with: buttered noodles and watercress salad.

Venison Patties

2 pounds ground venison
6 tablespoons red wine
8 strips bacon
  Melted butter
  Salt, pepper

Mix wine with the meat and refrigerate for 1–2 hours. Shape into 8 patties and wrap a strip of bacon around each, securing with toothpick. Brush patties with melted butter and sprinkle lightly with salt, pepper. Broil about 3 inches below flame or heat for about 15 minutes, turning once and brushing other sides with butter. Serves 4.
Serve with: broiled mushrooms and watercress salad.

Venison Liver and Bacon

2 pounds tender young deer liver, sliced ½ inch thick
   Milk
½ cup flour
1 teaspoon salt
½ teaspoon pepper
1 stick butter or margarine
8 slices bacon

Soak the liver slices in milk overnight in the refrigerator. Drain, pat dry, and roll slices in mixture of flour, salt, and pepper. Melt butter in a heavy skillet and sauté the slices over high heat, turning once, until lightly browned—about 5 minutes on each side. In a separate skillet, cook bacon until crisp over low heat. Drain bacon and serve on top of liver slices. Serves 4.

Serve with: Braised Endive (page 179) and Whole Fresh Cranberry Sauce (page 183).

Venison Swiss Steak

1 venison steak (2 pounds), 1 inch thick
3 tablespoons flour
½ stick butter or margarine
1 medium onion, coarsely chopped
1 small green pepper, seeded, coarsely chopped
1 stalk celery, sliced in ¼-inch rounds
1 cup canned plum tomatoes
2 cups beef consommé
1 teaspoon salt
3 crushed peppercorns

With a rolling pin or meat mallet, pound the flour into the meat on both sides. Over high heat melt butter in large skillet and quickly brown steak on both sides. Put all the vegetables in a tightly lidded pot or Dutch oven and place steak on top of them. Pour in the skillet drippings and the consommé. Add salt and peppercorns. Cover and simmer until meat is very tender—about 1½ hours. Serve with the vegetable gravy poured over. Serves 4.

Serve with: fluffy whipped potatoes or buttered broad noodles.

Tarragon Venison

8 slices cold cooked venison, each about 6 x 4 x ½ inches
2 tablespoons butter or margarine
2 tablespoons flour
1 cup light cream, slightly warmed
    Salt, pepper
2 tablespoons fresh tarragon, chopped fine
1 tablespoon brandy

Melt butter in deep skillet and blend in flour, stirring until golden brown. Over low heat, stir in the cream, mixing until smooth. When sauce begins to thicken, add salt and pepper to taste. Add remaining ingredients. Lay venison slices in sauce and heat through over low heat. Serves 4.
Serve with: wild, brown, or white rice or a mixture of half brown and half wild rice.

Venison Chops with Sour Cream Sauce

8 loin of venison chops, each 1 inch thick
¼ cup peanut oil
    Salt, pepper
2 cups Sour Cream Sauce (pages 162 and 163)

Trim fat from chops. Preheat broiler. Brush chops with oil and broil for 4 minutes. Turn, brush with oil, and broil 4 minutes more. Juice should be red when chops are fork-tested. Sprinkle with salt, pepper. Transfer to heated platter and pour hot sour cream sauce over all. Serves 4.
Serve with: buttered noodles and steamed fresh green beans.

Venisonburgers

2 pounds lean venison rump, twice-ground
1 medium onion, grated
½ cup fine dry bread crumbs
  Pinch of thyme
  Pinch of nutmeg
¼ teaspoon pepper
½ teaspoon salt
¼ teaspoon marjoram
¼ teaspoon garlic powder
1 egg, lightly beaten
2 tablespoons melted butter or margarine

Mix all ingredients except butter and form into 8 patties. Brush with melted butter and broil until golden brown—about 15 minutes—turning once and brushing again with butter. Serves 4.

Serve with: Sour Cream Sauce (pages 162 and 163) or currant jelly.

Note: Patties may be panfried in the butter over medium heat, taking about 8 minutes for each side.

Rich Venison Stew

3 pounds lean venison stew meat
2 cups White Wine Marinade (page 153)
  Salt, pepper
½ cup vegetable oil
1 large onion, peeled and chopped
1 large carrot, scraped and diced
2 shallots, peeled and coarsely chopped
1 clove garlic, minced
1½ cups white or red wine
2½ cups venison, beef, or chicken stock or bouillon
20 whole button mushrooms
20 whole pearl onions
8 thick (½-inch) slices bacon, diced and crisp-cooked
1 tablespoon flour mixed with 2 tablespoons water
  Chopped parsley for garnish

Marinate the meat for 1 or 2 days (depending on age and toughness) in a cool place. Drain and dry meat, reserving marinade. Sprinkle meat with salt, pepper. Heat oil in a Dutch oven or heavy kettle and cook onion and carrot until tender. Add and brown the meat. Remove excess fat and add shallots and garlic, turning and browning over medium heat. Add wine, 1 cup of the marinade, and enough stock to cover meat. Bring to boil, lower heat, cover, and simmer

Venison Loaf

for about 1½ hours. (If liquid cooks down too much, add more of the stock.) Remove meat and strain gravy, skimming off excess fat. Return meat to kettle, pour in strained gravy and mushrooms, onions, and diced cooked bacon. Add flour paste, if necessary, to thicken. Simmer for 25 minutes more or until meat is tender. Serve in casserole with parsley sprinkled over. Serves 6–8.

Serve with: butter-fried toast points.

Note: Recipe may be used for elk, rabbit, hare, and other wild or domestic meats unsuited to roasting.

2 pounds finely ground venison
½ pound good bulk sausage
1 large onion
2 stalks celery
¼ cup chopped parsley
¼ teaspoon thyme
1 cup bread crumbs made from day-old bread
1 cup canned plum tomatoes, drained
1 egg, lightly beaten
½ teaspoon salt
¼ teaspoon freshly ground black pepper
1 cup good catsup

Put venison, sausage, onion, and celery through meat grinder. Grind twice. Mix in glass or ceramic bowl with all the remaining ingredients except catsup. Turn into a buttered loaf pan. Pour catsup on top, spreading evenly to cover meat. Bake at 350° F. for about 1 hour or until done but still moist. Remove from pan. May be served hot or cold. Serves 6 or more.

Serve with: Bavarian Cabbage (page 180) or Stewed Apples (page 183).

Venison Meatballs

1 pound ground venison

4 tablespoons butter or margarine

3 tablespoons finely chopped onion

1½ cups soft bread crumbs soaked in ¾ cup milk

¼ teaspoon nutmeg

Pinch pepper

Pinch of baking powder

1½ teaspoons salt

1 egg, lightly beaten

1 cup venison or beef stock or consommé

1½ tablespoons flour mixed with 2 tablespoons water

In a large skillet, melt half the butter and sauté onion until golden. Add to the softened bread crumbs in a large mixing bowl. Add venison, nutmeg, pepper, baking powder, salt, and egg. Mix and form into 1-inch balls. Melt remaining butter in skillet and sauté meatballs until very lightly browned. Add stock, cover, simmer for 5 minutes, and remove meatballs to heated serving dish. Over medium heat, thicken the skillet liquids with the flour-water mixture and pour over meatballs. Makes about 3 dozen meatballs and serves 6.

Serve with: lingonberry or Whole Fresh Cranberry Sauce (page 183) and spinach noodles.

Roast Bear

1 7- to 8-pound bear loin, dressed, trimmed of all fat

4 cups Simple Marinade (page 150)

½ pound fat salt pork, cut in 1 x ¼ x ¼-inch strips, chilled

1 stick butter or margarine

3 medium onions, coarsely chopped

2 large carrots, scraped and coarsely chopped

3 medium stalks celery (tops included), coarsely chopped

2 large cloves garlic, minced

10 peppercorns, crushed

2 bay leaves

4 cups red wine

1 pint sour cream, warmed

½ teaspoon salt

¼ teaspoon freshly ground black pepper

Marinate meat in simple marinade for 4–8 days, depending on age and toughness. Drain; pat dry. Lard entire loin at 1- to 2-inch intervals. Melt butter in heavy skillet and sauté onions, carrots, celery, and garlic until limp and tender. Transfer skillet contents to deep roasting pan and place meat on top. Roast in preheated 450° F. oven for 10 minutes. Reduce heat to 350° and add peppercorns, bay leaves, and wine. Roast, basting every 15 minutes for 2 hours or until meat thermometer registers "well done" for beef.

Transfer roast to heated platter and keep warm. Strain pan juices through a coarse sieve and stir over low heat. Slowly add warmed sour cream. Add salt and pepper. Serve in sauceboat on side with roast. Serves 10–12.

Serve with: baked sweet potatoes and buttered lima beans or Baked Acorn Squash (page 181) and green beans.

Broiled Bear Steak

2 pounds bear steak, 1–1½ inches thick
Red Wine Marinade (page 153)
¼ cup vegetable oil
Salt
Freshly ground black pepper
Crushed dried sage
4 large onions, sliced thin
½ stick butter or margarine

Trim steak of all fat. Marinate for at least 24 hours and up to 3 days in red wine marinade, turning meat several times a day so that all surfaces are permeated. Drain; pat dry. Brush with oil on both sides and sprinkle liberally with salt, pepper, and sage. Broil for 15 minutes on each side— or until well done. Meanwhile sauté onions in butter until golden. Serve steak with onions on top. Serves 4.

Serve with: steamed buttered hominy and Wild Beach Plum Jelly (page 184).

Fillet of Bear

1 fillet of bear (about 6 pounds)
¼ pound larding strips, chilled
5 cups Big Game Marinade (page 155)
1 stick butter or margarine
4 small pickled onions
1 tablespoon capers
1 small shallot, chopped
3 sprigs fresh parsley
6 large fresh mushrooms, sliced
½ teaspoon salt
¼ teaspoon pepper
2 tablespoons butter or margarine
2 tablespoons flour

Lard the bear fillet and place in a crock, glass or ceramic pan. Pour over the marinade, cover, and refrigerate for 4 days, turning once a day to keep fillet coated. Drain, reserve marinade, and wipe fillet with damp cloth. Cut fillet in slices (about ½ inch thick). Melt butter in large, deep skillet and quickly sauté over high heat for 2 minutes on each side. Prepare sauce by placing in blender the onions, capers, shallot, parsley, mushrooms, salt, and pepper. Whirl till smooth (about 1 minute). Add 1 pint of the reserved marinade and whirl again till smooth (1 minute more). Melt butter in large skillet and blend in flour till smooth. Slowly add the blender mixture, stirring and cooking over high heat till mixture boils. Lower heat and add the bear fillet slices, cooking for about 30 minutes. Serves 8–10.

Serve with: Parsley Potato Dumplings (page 174) and Whole Fresh Cranberry Sauce (page 183).

Braised Bear Chops

4 lean bear chops, about 1 inch thick
1 teaspoon salt
1/4 teaspoon pepper
1/2 teaspoon paprika
1/2 teaspoon chervil or marjoram
3 cups hot beef stock or bouillon
1/4 cup wild rice soaked in water overnight
4 Spanish onion slices, 1/2 inch thick
1 cup sliced fresh mushrooms
1/2 cup sliced parsnip
2 tablespoons minced fresh parsley

Mix together the seasonings and rub chops on both sides with the mixture. Place chops close together in a deep, flame-proof casserole. Pour in 1 cup of the stock and simmer for 10 minutes. Spread rice over chops and lay an onion slice on each chop. Add the mushrooms and parsnip slices. Pour in remaining stock to cover all. Bring to boil, lower heat, cover tightly, and simmer for 40 minutes or until chops are tender and liquid is almost absorbed (remove lid 10 minutes before finishing cooking if liquid needs reduction). Dust with parsley. Serves 4.
Serve with: simple mixed green salad.

Bear Steak Cumberland

1 young bear steak, 1 1/2 inches thick (about 2 pounds)
1 1/2 sticks butter or margarine
2 tablespoons red currant jelly
1/2 cup port
1 tablespoon prepared hot mustard
1 teaspoon grated lemon peel
1 tablespoon shredded or slivered orange peel
1 teaspoon cognac or brandy

Melt butter over medium heat in a heavy iron skillet and sauté bear steak until tender but not rare (about 20 minutes). Put all remaining ingredients in a small saucepan, stirring over medium heat until piping hot but not boiling. Transfer steak to heated platter and pour sauce over. Serves 4.
Serve with: fried sweet potatoes and buttered green beans.

Braised Moose

2 pounds moose, cut in 1- or 2-inch cubes
2 tablespoons wine vinegar or red wine
½ cup flour
1 teaspoon salt
¼ teaspoon pepper
    Pinch cayenne
2 tablespoons salad oil
¼ teaspoon thyme
2 cups strong beef stock or bouillon
    Hot water
1 cup very small boiled onions
1 cup cooked peas

Sprinkle meat with the vinegar or wine. Mix together the flour, salt, pepper, and cayenne. Roll and coat meat in mixture. Heat oil in a Dutch oven or heavy pot with tight lid. Brown meat and add the thyme, stock, and enough hot water to cover. Simmer for about 2 hours, covered, or until meat is tender. Remove lid 15 minutes before finished. Add onions and peas just before serving and heat through. Serve in the pot gravy. Serves 4.

Serve with: Whipped Potatoes and Turnips (page 174).

Note: Recipe may also be used for caribou, buffalo, and bear meat as well.

Sweet-Sour Braised Moose

2 pounds moose cut up for stewing
2 cups beef stock or consommé
1 teaspoon salt
1 tablespoon sugar
½ teaspoon powdered cloves
½ teaspoon cinnamon
½ teaspoon allspice
    Pinch nutmeg
1 tablespoon butter or margarine
1 tablespoon flour
½ cup wine vinegar
½ cup finely chopped onion

In a heavy Dutch oven, put meat, stock, salt, sugar, cloves, cinnamon, allspice and nutmeg. Bring to boil, lower heat, and simmer, covered, until meat is tender—about 2 hours. During last half hour, melt butter in saucepan and blend in flour. Slowly add vinegar, stirring over medium heat, and blend till smooth. Add onion and simmer for 30 minutes. Drain stock from meat and add to sauce, cooking for 15 minutes longer. Add meat, heat through, and serve. Serves 4.

Serve with: Spaetzle (page 173).

Moose Steak in Casserole

6 pounds moose steaks, 2 inches thick (about 2 steaks)
4 tablespoons flour
3 tablespoons vegetable oil
¾ pound mushrooms, sliced thin
¾ cup beef stock
½ cup Madeira, port, vermouth, or sherry
1 teaspoon salt
6 crushed peppercorns

Coat steaks with flour and quickly brown in hot oil, searing both sides of meat. Place steaks in large flameproof casserole with snug lid. Add mushrooms, stock, wine, and seasonings. Cover and cook over moderate heat for 35 minutes (do not overcook). Cool and refrigerate in casserole. Skim off surplus fat and, when ready to serve, heat in a slow oven (325° F.) for about 25 minutes or until hot. Serve carved in thin strips with sauce on side. Serves 8–10.
Serve with: Parsley Potato Dumplings (page 174) or Spaetzle (page 173).

Moose Steak-and-Onions

1 2-inch young moose steak (about 3 pounds)
2 tablespoons fresh grated horseradish
½ cup vegetable oil
   Salt, pepper
4 large sweet onions, sliced thin
1½ sticks butter or margarine

Make 4 cuts at evenly spaced intervals in the steak—each about 2 x ½ inches. In each cut stuff ½ tablespoon of the horseradish. Preheat broiler. Brush steak with oil and broil cut side up for 6 minutes. Turn, brush again with oil, and broil 4 minutes. Turn twice more, brushing with oil each time, and broil 2–3 minutes more on each side. Meat should be rare. If medium-rare is desired, broil for several minutes more on each side, but do not overcook or steak will be tough. Sauté onions in the butter until limp and pale gold. Serve steak blanketed in the onions and cut in thin slices. Serves 6.
Serve with: Currant Jelly Sauce (page 161).

Roast Haunch of Antelope

1 haunch (leg or ham) of antelope (10–12 pounds), trimmed of
   all fat, skin
½ pound fat salt pork cut in larding strips, chilled
5 cups Big Game Marinade (page 155)
¼ cup olive oil
1 stick melted butter or margarine

Marinate the haunch overnight in the marinade. Drain, wipe dry, and rub with olive oil. Place in roaster and roast at 350° F. for 12 minutes per pound for rare, 15 minutes per pound for medium. Baste during roasting every 15 minutes by brushing haunch with melted butter and the pan drippings. Serves 8–10.

Serve with: Currant Jelly Sauce (page 161).

Note: Recipe also good for leg or haunch of venison or elk.

Broiled Peccary Chops

6 peccary loin chops, each about 1 inch thick
2¼ cups Fatty Game Marinade (page 152)
   Salt, pepper
¼ cup bacon drippings or vegetable oil

Marinate chops for about 4 hours in the marinade, turning once every hour. Drain; pat dry. Sprinkle with salt and pepper. Heat drippings or oil and sear and brown chops on both sides over high heat. Remove from pan and place under broiler, finishing cooking by broiling for about 7 minutes on each side. Serves 6.

Serve with: mashed turnips, applesauce or stewed apricots.

Roast Wild Boar

1 haunch (about 4 pounds) of young wild boar

1 bottle red wine

1 teaspoon sugar

12 juniper berries

8 peppercorns

¼ cup cider vinegar

2 tablespoons lemon juice

½ teaspoon salt

2 bay leaves

¼ teaspoon dried thyme

1 medium onion, peeled, stuck with 3 cloves

3 medium carrots, sliced thin

1 stick butter or margarine

Wipe the meat and place it in a deep ceramic bowl or crock with a marinade made of a mixture of all the ingredients (except butter). Set in a cool place for 48 hours or longer, turning meat frequently so that marinade covers all surfaces. Drain and wipe dry, reserving marinade. Rub butter all over the meat and place in a roasting pan. Pour in a half inch of the strained marinade. Roast in preheated 450° F. oven for 15 minutes or until brown, turning meat once. Reduce heat to 300° and roast, basting every half hour with remaining marinade, for 1½ hours or until tender (a meat thermometer should register "well done" for pork). Transfer to heated platter and serve with the pan gravy in a sauceboat. Serves 4–6.

Serve with: Whole Fresh Cranberry Sauce (page 183), baked sweet potatoes.

Note: A loin of fresh ham may be substituted for the boar.

Reindeer Chops

6 double-cut loin reindeer chops
1/4 cup olive or peanut oil
1 tablespoon chopped fresh fennel leaves
6 peppercorns, crushed in a mortar
1 tablespoon chopped fresh parsley
  Pinch paprika
1/2 teaspoon salt
1/4 cup red wine
  Juice of 1 lemon
1/2 stick butter or margarine
1/2 cup tart red currant jelly or Wild Beach Plum Jelly
    (page 184)
1/4 cup fresh grated horseradish

Mix together the oil, fennel, peppercorns, parsley, paprika, salt, wine, and lemon juice. Pour over chops in shallow glass or ceramic dish and turn chops so all surfaces are coated with the mixture. Allow to stand in cool place for about 4 hours, turning and coating chops every hour. Preheat broiler when ready to cook chops. Wipe chops thoroughly with paper towels and smear both sides of each chop with the butter. Broil for 2 minutes only on each side. Serve at once with the jelly and horseradish mixed together on the side. Serves 6.
Serve with: boiled new potatoes and new peas.

Stewed Goat, Spanish Style

4 pounds young goat (kid) meat, cubed for stewing
  Juice of 2 large limes
2 large cloves garlic, mashed
1 tablespoon oregano
1/2 teaspoon pepper
1 tablespoon salt
1 tablespoon vinegar
2 dozen pitted green olives
2 tablespoons capers
3 large onions, sliced thin
2 large bay leaves, crumbled
1 dozen pitted prunes
1 cup chicken stock or water
1 cup sweet red wine
1/4 cup sugar

Place meat in glass or ceramic bowl and sprinkle with the lime juice. Refrigerate, covered, overnight. Place meat in a Dutch oven and add all ingredients except the wine and sugar. Bring to boil over high heat and boil for 10 minutes. Cover, lower heat to medium, and cook for 1 hour. Add wine and sugar, cover and continue cooking for 1 more hour or until meat is tender. Serves 8.
Serve with: baked sweet potatoes or fried plantains.

Caribou Stew

3 pounds caribou, cut up for stew

Juice of 1 lemon and grated peel from 1 lemon

1½ teaspoons salt

2 teaspoons chili powder

½ cup flour

3 tablespoons olive oil

3 cups hot beef stock or bouillon

1 cup chopped stuffed olives

Sprinkle meat with lemon juice and let stand for 1 hour at room temperature. Mix together the salt, chili powder, and flour and coat meat on all surfaces with the mixture. Heat oil in heavy pot or Dutch oven and brown the meat. Add stock to cover meat. Add grated lemon peel. Cover tightly and simmer for 1½ hours. Remove lid and continue to simmer for 15 minutes more or until meat is tender and juices are reduced. Stir in olives. Serves 6.

Serve with: Spaetzle (page 173).

Note: Recipe may also be used for bear, moose, elk, antelope, or tough cuts of deer.

Roast Buffalo

1 buffalo eye roast (about 6 pounds) or buffalo hump roast

5 cups Big Game Marinade (page 155)

Marinate meat, turning every few hours, for 1 or 2 days in the marinade. Drain. Reserve marinade and strain it. Wipe roast dry with a damp cloth and place in roasting pan. Place in preheated 425° F. oven and roast for 15 minutes. Lower heat to 350° and continue roasting with 1 cup of the strained marinade poured over for 1½ hours or until meat thermometer registers "rare" for beef. Continue roasting until desired degree of doneness. Meat should be served no more than "medium rare" for best flavor. During roasting, baste with additional marinade. Transfer to heated platter and serve sliced as for roast beef. Serves 10.

Serve with: roast new potatoes and Fruit Sauce (page 163).

Note: Elk, deer, and reindeer may be substituted for the buffalo or bison.

Pot Roast of Buffalo

1 young buffalo rump roast (about 5½–6 pounds)
¼ pound chilled fat salt pork larding strips
5 cups Big Game Marinade (page 155)
¼ cup lard or margarine
1 tablespoon flour
2 cups beef stock or strong bouillon
1 tablespoon tomato paste
2 tablespoons flour dissolved in 3 tablespoons cold marinade

Insert larding strips at 2-inch intervals all over the meat. Put in crock or ceramic or glass bowl and pour marinade over. Let stand, covered, in a cool place for 1 or 2 days, turning meat every few hours so all surfaces are permeated. Remove meat and reserve marinade. Wipe meat dry with paper towels. Heat lard in large, deep skillet or heavy pot and brown meat all over. Sprinkle with the flour and add stock to cover. Add 2 cups of the marinade and the tomato paste and cook, covered, over medium heat for about 1 hour or until meat is tender. Remove meat to heated platter and keep warm. Skim fat from pot and strain juices into saucepan. Thicken with the flour-marinade if necessary. Slice meat and pour some of gravy over it; serve remaining gravy in a sauceboat. Serves 10–12.
Serve with: candied yams or sweet potatoes.

Tender young rabbits have light, fine-textured meat with little or no gamey flavor (thanks to the nature of their diets). Because they taste very much like chicken and can be cooked like chicken, most chicken recipes will work with rabbit as a substitute. Unlike the hare, they do not require marinating or long cooking for best results. An old rabbit, however, needs all the attention it can get to render it palatable. The average young wild rabbit weighs 3–4 pounds, older ones (jackrabbits) may weigh as much as 10 pounds. Domestic, farm-raised rabbits average 2 pounds in weight.

While the terms "rabbit" and "hare" are used interchangeably in some parts of the country, the true rabbit is a cottontail, brush, marsh, Idaho pygmy, or other and is smaller and much tenderer than the hare.

Wild hare is usually dark-meated and may weigh from 4 to 12 pounds. One of the largest species is the snowshoe hare. The flesh of the hare is pleasantly gamey in flavor and, depending on its age, can be tough. It is best braised, stewed, and roasted if well marinated. An excellent food, prized by hunters, it is available at specialty butcher shops in domestic form. The farm-raised variety is tenderer, less gamey, and may be roasted without premarinating.

Squirrels proliferate throughout the United States, the most prevalent being the gray squirrel. Other edible species include the tassel-eared or Abert pine squirrel, the fox squirrel, and the California gray. The white meat of this little animal is tender, delicately flavored, and, when young, is excellent broiled or fried. Like the young rabbit it resembles chicken and may substitute for that bird in any of its many recipes. Older squirrels are tough, but celebrated in the popular Brunswick Stew (page 54). A gray squirrel weighs slightly more than a pound on the average; a fox squirrel averages about 2 pounds.

Muskrat, or "marsh rabbit" as it is nicknamed in the South, is a very clean animal and a vegetarian. Its flesh is dark, fine-grained, and strongly flavored. A popular delicacy in the marsh country, it may be stewed, broiled, dipped in batter and fried, or braised. But it must first be soaked overnight in a saline solution, then parboiled if it is to be broiled. Muskrat fanciers declare it at its best when fried.

Woodchuck, better known as the groundhog to non-hunters and a pest to the farmer, is often overlooked as a food. Strong-flavored, it, too, should be soaked overnight in salt water, and if it is an old one, it should be parboiled before cooking in other ways. Old-timers like it ground for woodchuckburgers and meat loaves, but a young woodchuck is excellent when disjointed and roasted.

Both raccoon and opossum have a porklike flavor and,

properly prepared, make excellent eating as any Southerner knows. Not available in game markets or specialty butcher shops, these animals are truly wild. The opossum is at its best after the first frost, and fanciers of its meat recommend that the animal be hung outdoors for a few days when the weather is freezing. The procedure for preparing it and raccoon is the same as for woodchuck. Recipes for these three small game animals are interchangeable. All three are fatty and the fat should be removed before cooking.

Hare in White Wine Sauce

1 hare (4½–5 pounds), drawn and dressed, cut in serving pieces
1 stick butter or margarine
1 tablespoon vegetable oil
1 jigger brandy, warmed
3 cups dry white wine
¼ teaspoon dried thyme
12 whole small white onions, peeled
½ teaspoon crushed dried rosemary
12 medium mushrooms, sliced, stems included
12 small pork sausages, cooked until browned

Melt half the stick of butter in a deep iron skillet. Add the oil and, when hot, brown the hare on all surfaces. Remove from heat, pour the brandy over all and ignite. When flames die, return skillet to heat and add the wine and thyme. Simmer, turning the meat occasionally, for 1 hour. Meanwhile, melt remaining butter in another skillet and sauté the onions with the rosemary until golden on all surfaces. Add the mushrooms and the sausages and simmer for 5–10 minutes. Just before serving, add this mixture to the hare, mixing all together by turning meat gently. Cook 5 more minutes over low heat. Transfer to a heated platter or a casserole. Serves 4–6.
Serve with: fluffy white rice or wild rice.

Saddle of Hare

1 saddle of hare (2–2½ pounds), dressed, split in 4 pieces
1 clove garlic, halved
   Butter
2 teaspoons salt
½ teaspoon paprika
   Freshly ground black pepper
6 slices bacon, cut in half
1 pint sour cream, warmed
1 cup seedless white grapes

Wipe and dry meat. Rub it all over with the cut sides of the garlic. Sprinkle with salt, paprika, and pepper. Place in roasting pan and cover with bacon. Bake at 350° F. for 45 minutes or until tender. Remove to heated platter. Skim excess fat from pan and stir in the sour cream and grapes. Cook, stirring, over low heat for 4–5 minutes and pour over meat. Serves 2–3.
Serve with: Braised Endive (page 179).

Fillet of Hare

1 fillet of hare (about 1 pound)
White Wine Marinade (page 153)
1/4 pound chilled fat salt pork
2 tablespoons butter
3/4 cup heavy cream, warmed
1 tablespoon lemon juice
Salt, pepper

Marinate the fillet for about 3 hours in a ceramic or glass dish. Cut larding strips and enough thin slices of fat to cover the fillet. Drain and wipe the fillet. Lard it at 2-inch intervals. Cover with the fat slices and place in roasting pan. Add butter and roast in preheated oven at 450° F. for 20 minutes or until meat thermometer reaches 150° or "very rare" for beef. Transfer fillet to heated serving plate and keep warm. Skim excess fat from pan and stir in the cream. Heat through, stirring, and bring to boil. Add lemon juice. Add salt, pepper to taste. Pour very hot over the fillet which has been cut across the grain in four equal pieces. Serves 2.
Serve with: Baked Stuffed Mushrooms (page 182) and toast points fried in butter.

Sweet-Sour Hare

1 hare (4–5 pounds), dressed, liver and blood reserved
1 1/4 sticks butter or margarine
Salt, pepper
1 tablespoon flour
4 cups red wine
1 tablespoon sugar
2 tablespoons chopped fresh parsley
1 bay leaf, crumbled
1/4 teaspoon thyme
3 medium onions, sliced thin

Have butcher reserve the blood and cut hare into serving-size pieces. Melt butter in large, deep skillet. Sprinkle meat with salt, pepper. Brown it quickly on all sides in the hot butter. Sprinkle with flour and add the liver, chopped fine. Turn and cook until liver is lightly browned. Remove meat. Add wine and hare blood (about 1/2 cup) to skillet, stirring over medium heat. Add sugar and all remaining ingredients. Return meat to skillet. Bring to boil, cover, and simmer for 45 minutes. If not tender and cooked through, continue simmering for another 15–20 minutes. Transfer meat to heated platter. Strain sauce and heat through. Pour over meat. Serves 6.
Serve with: Brussels Sprouts with Chestnuts (page 177).

Jugged Hare

1 hare (5–6 pounds) cut in 8 pieces
2 cups red wine, port, or claret
2 large onions, sliced
1 tablespoon mixed pickling spices
1 teaspoon salt
1/8 teaspoon black pepper
1 stick butter or margarine
1 herb bouquet (parsley, thyme, bay leaf)
2 cups hot bouillon or beef stock
Instant flour

Place hare in large bowl and add wine, onions, spices, salt, pepper. Let stand in refrigerator, turning occasionally, for 1 or 2 days. Then remove, pat dry, and reserve marinade. Melt butter in heatproof casserole; brown hare on all sides. Remove from heat. Pour marinade over all. Add herb bouquet and bouillon. Cover and bake at 350° F. for 2–3 hours. During last half hour, sprinkle with the flour and stir. Continue baking, uncovered. Thicken and strain gravy. Pour over. Serves 6.
Serve with: red currant jelly, Braised Celery (page 179).

Terrine of Hare

1 hare (3–3½ pounds), boned, cut in 2-inch pieces
½ pound veal, coarse ground
1 pound pork, coarse ground
½ cup cold chicken stock or consommé
1 cup port wine
1 tablespoon cognac
2 tablespoons minced fresh parsley
½ teaspoon basil
¼ teaspoon thyme
Pinch cloves
¼ teaspoon freshly ground black pepper
½ teaspoon salt
8–10 slices lean bacon
Piecrust dough for one-crust pie
1 egg yolk, lightly beaten

Mix together in a ceramic or glass bowl all ingredients except bacon, piecrust, and egg yolk. Cover and refrigerate for 2 hours. Line a heatproof earthenware casserole with the bacon strips, overlapping them about ½ inch. Put hare mixture in lined casserole and top with crimped pastry crust. Slash small vents for steam and bake at 350° F. for 2 hours. Brush with egg; bake till brown. Serves 6.
Serve with: Spicy White Cabbage (page 180).

Tarragon Rabbit

2 young rabbits (2–3 pounds each), cut in serving-size pieces
Flour
Salt
Pepper
1½ sticks butter or margarine
1½ cups dry white wine
1 teaspoon dried tarragon leaves or 1½ tablespoons chopped fresh tarragon
2 teaspoons instant flour

Dust meat with flour and sprinkle with salt, pepper. Melt butter in large, heavy skillet and lightly brown the meat. Lower heat, add wine and cover tightly. Simmer until tender—about 45 minutes. Sprinkle with tarragon. Cook 5 minutes more. Sprinkle with flour, stir, and, when sauce is thickened, serve immediately. Serves 4–6.
Serve with: crisp shoestring potatoes.

Fried Rabbit

2 wild rabbits (2–3 pounds each), cut in serving pieces
Lemon juice
Salt, pepper
¼ teaspoon dried oregano
4 tablespoons milk
2 eggs, lightly beaten
½ cup flour
½ cup fine bread crumbs
Peanut oil

Put rabbit pieces in water to cover with a little lemon juice (half a lemon) and parboil for 10 minutes. Drain, pat dry, and sprinkle with salt, pepper, oregano. Combine milk and egg. Dip rabbit in flour, then in egg, and then in bread crumbs. Heat ½ inch of oil in large skillet till a cube of bread turns golden in 1 minute. Brown rabbit on all sides. Lower heat and cook till tender (about 20 minutes). Drain and serve at once. Serves 4–6.
Serve with: Gooseberry Sauce (page 164).

Baked Rabbit

2 small rabbits, backs and ribs removed, cut in serving pieces
2 eggs, lightly beaten
1 cup dry bread crumbs
2 tablespoons butter or margarine
2 tablespoons peanut oil
1 pint chicken stock, consommé, or bouillon
2 medium onions stuck with a clove each

Dip rabbit pieces in egg, then coat with bread crumbs. Heat butter and oil in large skillet and brown the meat on all sides. Transfer skillet contents to shallow roasting pan and pour in enough stock nearly to cover meat. Add onions and bake at 350° F. until meat is tender—about 1 hour. Serves 4–6.
Serve with: **Parsley Potato Dumplings** (page 174) or other favorite dumplings.

Irish Rabbit Pasties

1 large rabbit, quartered
Salt
1 cup Basic White Sauce (page 157)
¼ cup dry bread crumbs
3 slices cold boiled ham, diced
½ teaspoon grated lemon rind
4 teaspoons minced fresh parsley
Short pastry for large two-crust pie
1 tablespoon melted butter

Put rabbit in heavy saucepan with salted water to cover. Bring to boil, lower heat, cover, and simmer until very tender and meat falls from bones—about 1½ hours. Drain; remove all meat and cut in ½-inch cubes. Heat white sauce and add bread crumbs, ham, lemon rind, and parsley. Heat through and add rabbit meat. Set aside to cool. Meanwhile roll out pastry on floured board to ⅛-inch thickness and cut 12 6-inch circles from dough. Place a mound of the rabbit mixture in center of half of the circles, dividing mixture equally among them. Place remaining circles on top and crimp edges together. Brush pies with melted butter and cut V vents for steam in each. Bake at 450° F. for 15–20 minutes or until light brown. Serves 4.
Note: May be served hot or cold as a luncheon snack.

Apricot Rabbit

2 small rabbits cut in serving-size pieces
1 8-ounce bottle creamy Russian dressing
1 cup apricot jam
¼ cup apricot liqueur
1 package dry onion soup mix

Place rabbit pieces in a baking pan or casserole large enough to hold them in a single layer. Mix all remaining ingredients thoroughly and pour over the rabbit. Bake in preheated oven at 350° F. for about 1 hour or until meat is tender. Baste every 15 minutes during baking. Serves 4. *Serve with:* Rice Pilaf (page 171).

Prune-Stuffed Rabbit

2 2-pound rabbits or 1 4-pound hare, dressed whole
  Salt, pepper
1 stick butter or margarine, melted
3 cups croutons or 3 cups herb-seasoned dry stuffing mix
1¼ cups pitted, chopped, cooked prunes
½ cup vegetable oil
½ cup red wine
½ teaspoon freshly ground black pepper
½ teaspoon salt

Wipe rabbits dry inside and out. Sprinkle cavities with salt, pepper. Combine butter, croutons, and prunes, tossing all lightly together. Fill cavities and close with skewers or butcher's cord laced over poultry pins. Spit on rotisserie and roast for 1½ hours, basting every 15 minutes with a mixture of the oil, wine, pepper, and salt. Serves 4–6. *Serve with:* hot applesauce.
Note: Stuffing may also be used for roast pheasant or turkey.

Hasenpfeffer

2 rabbits, cut in serving-size pieces
2 cups vinegar
2 cups red wine
2 cups chopped onion
2 teaspoons salt
8 juniper berries, crushed
½ teaspoon powdered cloves
¼ teaspoon dried thyme
2 bay leaves, crumbled
½ teaspoon crushed peppercorns
    Flour
½ cup vegetable oil
1 cup strong chicken stock or undiluted canned consommé
1 tablespoon sugar
1 tablespoon butter or margarine kneaded with 1 tablespoon
    flour

Mix together in a large ceramic or glass bowl the vinegar, wine, onion, salt, juniper berries, cloves, thyme, bay leaves, and peppercorns. Add and turn rabbit pieces in the mixture. Refrigerate for 24–48 hours, turning rabbit several times so that all pieces are permeated with the marinade. Drain, reserving marinade, and dry pieces. Roll rabbit pieces in flour. Heat oil in large, deep skillet and brown rabbit on all sides. Pour off oil. Add reserved marinade, stock, and sugar. Cover and simmer gently for 1 hour or until meat is tender. Remove meat to heated platter. Add the butter-flour mixture, stir over medium heat until thickened, strain and pour over rabbit. Serves 6.
Serve with: Parsley Potato Dumplings (page 174).
Note: A large hare may be substituted for the rabbits.

Rabbit in Wine Sauce

2 small rabbits, cut in serving-size pieces
½ stick butter or margarine
2 tablespoons olive or peanut oil
6 slices bacon, diced
1½ cups pearl onions
2 tablespoons flour
2 cups sweet red wine
½ teaspoon thyme
1 bay leaf, crumbled
¼ teaspoon pepper
1 tablespoon chopped fresh parsley
   Pinch nutmeg
2 cups water
2 tablespoons tomato paste
1 large clove garlic, minced fine
½ pound fresh mushrooms, sliced thin

Melt butter and oil in Dutch oven and slowly brown rabbits on all sides. In a skillet, cook and brown the bacon along with the pearl onions. Set aside. When rabbit is browned, sprinkle with flour. Add all ingredients except mushrooms. Cover tightly and place in 350° F. oven for 1½ hours. Add mushrooms during last 15 minutes. Serves 4–6.
Serve with: parsley-dusted tiny boiled potatoes.

Crisp-Fried Rabbit

2 young rabbits (about 2 pounds each), disjointed and cut in serving pieces
2 tablespoons vinegar
1 teaspoon salt
½ teaspoon pepper
2 eggs, lightly beaten
1½ cups fine, dry bread crumbs
2 cups peanut oil or lard

Put meat in large pot and cover with water. Add vinegar and boil, covered, for 10–15 minutes. Drain and pat pieces of meat dry. Sprinkle with the salt, pepper. Dip each piece first in egg and then in bread crumbs, coating all surfaces. Heat oil or lard until a cube of bread browns in 1 minute. Fry coated meat pieces in the hot fat until golden brown. Drain on paper towels and, when all pieces are done, place under broiler for a minute on each side to ensure crispness. (Or place in a 250° F. oven as pieces are done and drained.) Serves 6.
Serve with: Spicy White Cabbage (page 180).

Rabbit in Mustard Sauce

2 small rabbits, disjointed, cut in serving-size pieces
Flour
Salt, pepper
Pinch nutmeg
1 stick butter or margarine
4 slices very lean bacon, chopped fine
6 green onions (tops removed), chopped fine
1 clove garlic, minced
1 tablespoon chopped fresh parsley
1 bay leaf, crumbled
1/4 teaspoon thyme
1/2 cup white wine
1/2 cup water
2 egg yolks, lightly beaten
1/2 pint heavy cream
2 tablespoons sweet prepared mustard

Wipe and dry meat. Dust each piece with flour and sprinkle with salt, pepper, and nutmeg. Melt butter in a Dutch oven or large, heavy skillet and add bacon. Brown meat over medium heat. Then add onions, garlic, parsley, bay leaf, and thyme. Pour the wine and water over all, cover, and simmer until meat is tender, about 45 minutes. Transfer meat to heated serving dish and keep warm. Skim excess fat from pot and strain remaining juices (forcing through sieve with back of spoon) into a saucepan. Stir the egg yolks into the cream along with the mustard. Add to the strained sauce and cook, stirring, over low heat until heated through. Pour over meat. Serves 4–6.

Serve with: Spaetzle (page 173) or buttered noodles.

Broiled Squirrel

2 plump young squirrels, dressed, split lengthwise
  Salt, pepper
¼ cup melted butter, margarine or bacon fat

Wipe and dry the squirrel halves. Sprinkle with salt, pepper. Preheat broiler and place meat skin side down on rack. Brush with the butter or fat. Broil 8 inches from heat for 15 minutes, basting frequently to keep meat moist. Turn, brush with butter or fat again, and continue to broil for 15 minutes more, constantly basting. Meat should be cooked through (as for chicken). Serves 4.

Serve with: Stewed Apples (page 183) and crisp bacon slices.
Note: This method of broiling is also suitable for young rabbit.

Brunswick Stew

1 large squirrel, dressed
2 quarts boiling water
1 cup whole kernel corn
1 cup lima beans
2 large potatoes
½ large onion
1½ teaspoons salt
½ teaspoon black pepper
2 cups plum tomatoes
1½ teaspoons sugar
¼ cup butter or margarine

Cut squirrel into 8 serving pieces. Add all ingredients except sugar, butter, and tomatoes to the boiling water and simmer for 2 hours. Add tomatoes and sugar; simmer 1 hour. Add butter; simmer 10 minutes. Bring to boil and remove from heat. Serves 4.

Serve with: hot, crusty French bread.

Honey-Cider Squirrel

2 young squirrels, dressed whole and halved
½ cup thick honey
1 pint apple cider
2 crushed bay leaves
1 tablespoon cornstarch mixed with 2 tablespoons water

Wipe squirrel halves dry and lay on broiler rack. Coat completely with honey. Broil about 6 inches from heat for 8 minutes. Turn, coat again with honey, and broil 8 minutes more. Transfer to large, shallow baking dish or bottom of roaster. Pour in the cider and add bay leaves. Place in preheated 350° F. oven and roast for 1 hour or until meat is well done. Transfer to serving platter and keep warm. Strain pan juices into saucepan over medium heat and thicken with the cornstarch mixture. Serve on side. Serves 4.
Serve with: crisp shoestring potatoes and green salad.

Applejack Squirrel

3 squirrels (1 pound each) cut in serving pieces
Flour
Salt, pepper
¼ cup diced bacon
1½ cups applejack
2 tablespoons butter
1 cup cream, warmed
1 tablespoon butter
2 teaspoons instant flour

Wipe meat dry, then dust it with flour, salt, pepper. In a large skillet, fry bacon until it is golden, but do not brown. Add meat and brown. Pour in applejack, cover, and simmer until meat is tender and liquid almost evaporated. Add butter and stir. Remove meat to platter. Add cream to pan. Stir in remaining butter. Sprinkle with instant flour. Continue to heat, stirring, until thickened. Pour over meat. Serves 6.
Serve with: Stewed Apples (page 183) and baked yams.

Squirrel Fricassee

1 large squirrel, disjointed, cut in serving-size pieces
½ cup flour
½ teaspoon salt
¼ teaspoon pepper
4 slices fatty bacon, chopped fine
1 small onion, chopped fine
2 teaspoons lemon juice
1 large apple, cored, diced
1½ cups chicken stock or consommé

Mix together the flour, salt, and pepper. Roll meat in mixture and coat evenly. In a large, heavy skillet, slowly fry the bacon. Remove bacon and reserve. Turn up heat and brown the meat in the bacon fat. Sprinkle with onion and lemon juice. Return bacon to pan and add apple and stock. Cover and simmer for 2–2½ hours over low heat or until meat is tender. Serve hot in a casserole with pan juices poured over. Serves 2–4.
Serve with: buttered hominy.

Squirrel Gumbo

2 young squirrels, cut in serving-size pieces
¼ cup vegetable oil or bacon fat
1 large green pepper, seeded, sliced
1 sweet red pepper, seeded, sliced
2 large stalks celery, diced
1 medium onion, diced
2 tablespoons chopped parsley
1½ cups fresh okra, cut in ½-inch rounds or 1 package frozen
        okra, thawed and drained
3 pints chicken stock or consommé
2 large tomatoes, peeled, sliced, or 2 cups canned
1 small can (6-ounce) shoepeg corn or other
¾ cup cooked white rice
1½ teaspoons filé powder dissolved in 1 tablespoon water

In a Dutch oven, heat oil and brown the meat. Add peppers, celery, and onion and cook, stirring, over medium heat until vegetables are limp. Add parsley, okra (if fresh), and stock. Cover and simmer until meat is tender (40–50 minutes). Remove meat and bone it, if desired, and return to stew. Add tomatoes, corn, rice, and okra (if frozen). Simmer 5 minutes. Stir in filé powder. Serves 6.
Serve with: crusty, hot French bread and a cruet of sherry to be added to stew as desired.

Roast Raccoon

1 raccoon (4–5 pounds), dressed whole, all fat removed
4 large green apples, quartered
2 cups beef or chicken stock
4 wide strips fat salt pork, cut ¼ inch thick
4 medium onions, peeled
2 tablespoons instant minced chives
2 tablespoons chopped fresh parsley
1 tablespoon instant flour
   Salt, pepper

If the raccoon is excessively fatty, boil it in salt water to cover (1 tablespoon salt to 1 quart water) for 20–30 minutes. Drain; pat dry. Place apples in cavity and skewer together or sew up. Place breast side down in roasting pan. Add stock and cover meat with the fat strips. Roast slowly in a 325° F. oven until tender (about 2½ hours), basting every 30 minutes with the pan juices. During last hour, place onions in pan and, during last half hour, remove fat strips. When done, transfer to heated platter and keep warm. Skim excess fat from pan juices and add chives, parsley, and flour. Stir over medium heat till thickened and serve on side as gravy. Serves 6-8.
Serve with: baked yams or candied sweet potatoes.

Stewed Woodchuck

1 plump woodchuck (groundhog), cut in 3–4 pieces
½ cup vinegar
2 teaspoons salt
2 tablespoons baking soda
1 large onion, sliced thin
½ teaspoon pepper
1 bay leaf
4 whole allspice
1 tablespoon chopped fresh parsley
   Dash Worcestershire sauce
2 teaspoons flour mixed with 2 tablespoons water

In a crock or large ceramic or glass bowl, cover meat with water and add vinegar and salt. Let stand overnight. Drain meat and place in heavy kettle. Again cover with water and add the soda. Bring to boil and continue to boil for 20 minutes. Drain. Rinse kettle and put meat in it. Cover with water and add onion, pepper, bay leaf, allspice, parsley, and Worcestershire sauce. Simmer for about 1 hour or until meat is tender, but not falling from the bones. Transfer meat to heated platter and keep warm. Reduce remaining liquid in kettle by boiling down to about 1½ cups. Thicken with the flour mixture and pour over the meat. Serves 4–6.
Serve with: stewed tomatoes.

Roast Opossum

1 young opossum
2 teaspoons salt
4 large red chili peppers, seeded, chopped
1 large onion, chopped
6 peppercorns, crushed in a mortar
8 strips fatty bacon
6 medium sweet potatoes or 4 large yams, peeled and sliced
   ½ inch thick

Put opossum in large kettle with water to cover. Add salt, red peppers, onion, and peppercorns. Simmer for 30 minutes. Drain meat; reserve liquid. Put meat in a roasting pan. Cover with bacon strips. Continue cooking kettle liquid, boiling over high heat until about 2½ cups remain. Pour this over the meat and roast in preheated 350° F. oven for 30 minutes, basting every 10 minutes. Arrange potatoes or yams around the meat and continue to roast for 30 minutes more or until meat is tender and potatoes or yams are done. Serves 4–6.
Serve with: cooked turnip greens.

Muskrat in Onion Sauce

1 plump marsh rabbit or muskrat
2 tablespoons salt
2 quarts water
½ cup flour
1 teaspoon salt
½ teaspoon pepper
6 strips fatty bacon, chopped
1 can (10½-ounce) undiluted onion soup
1 cup sour cream, warmed

Soak whole muskrat in salt and water in a crock or glass bowl overnight. Drain; cut in serving-size pieces. Mix flour, salt, and pepper together and roll meat in mixture, coating all pieces. In a deep, heavy skillet or Dutch oven, fry the bacon until transparent and light brown. Add the meat and brown on all sides. Add the soup and sour cream. Stir. Lower heat, cover tightly, and simmer for about 1 hour or until meat is tender, but not falling from bones. Serves 4.
Serve with: mashed potatoes and steamed, buttered carrots.
Note: Recipe is suitable for rabbit, omitting the overnight soaking step.

While pheasant, grouse, and quail are considered "the big three" by gourmets judging the upland birds, there are many equally fine epicurean treats to be found among the doves, pigeons, partridges, ptarmigans, woodcocks, and those noblest American birds, the wild turkeys. It is, however, "the big three" that can be found most readily in the market. Doves and pigeons (and squabs), as well as wild turkey (often smoked), can be ordered in advance through some purveyors. Pheasant in the specialty butcher shop is pen-raised and the young pigeons or squabs are, of course, domesticated.

The most tender of all these birds is the dove. The pigeon is larger and tougher. Both are plentiful. Of some 475 species of these dark-meated creatures, three are best known in the United States as wild game birds: mourning dove, found in every state; the white-winged dove of the South and Southeast; and the Western band-tailed pigeon. Mourning doves are regarded as songbirds in most of the Northeast, but in other parts of the country, sportsmen find them swift targets, challenging shots, and excellent eating. Older, tougher pigeons are best when braised; younger ones may be roasted. Doves are more delicate and are excellent when simply split and grilled or sautéed as well as when simmered in a casserole.

The quail is another abundant game bird. More than twenty-two million annually grace the tables at epicurean feasts, and they are raised and found throughout the country. The five major groups are the crested, plumed, spotted, Western and Eastern upland quail. There are numerous subspecies in each of these, including the popular bobwhite, the desert, Massena, scaled, mountain, and valley quail. The bobwhite is the most prolific and abounds in the Southeast. A small bird, averaging 5½–6 ounces, it is plump with delicately flavored, somewhat dry meat. It is best sautéed, broiled, or baked with frequent basting or heavy barding.

The showiest of birds is the cock pheasant (the hen is squattier and drabber by comparison), and it is prized for its fine-grained, densely packed, white-meated breasts (the legs are dark-meated). As with most wild game birds, the pheasant needs liberal larding or barding and frequent basting to keep the meat moist as it bakes or roasts. Older birds should be braised or stewed.

Purists say that there are only two true partridges in this country. And there is confusion. In the South, the name partridge is applied to several kinds of quail; in the North, the ruffed grouse is sometimes called a partridge. The North American partridge is a fairly recent import. The Hungarian partridge or Hun was introduced here some fifty years ago from Eastern Europe. Its range is Wisconsin, parts of Oregon, Idaho, Montana, Illinois, Minnesota, the Dakotas, and here and there in some of the Eastern states. The chukar partridge—originally from the region around the Himalayas—is found in California, Minnesota, Nevada, North Dakota, Washington, and Wyoming. The average bird, weighing 10–14 ounces, is best roasted or broiled. Older ones should be braised or stewed.

The best-known American grouse is the wide-ranging ruffed grouse, found from Minnesota through the New England States and from Pennsylvania to northern Georgia and Alabama. Among others widely distributed in the country are Franklin's grouse, spruce grouse, sharp-tailed grouse, and pinnated grouse (also known as prairie chicken). In the grouse family are also the feather-footed ptarmigans, found in the Rocky Mountains. All are excellent food except for the sage grouse which feeds heavily on sage buds and may prove distasteful to some palates (speedy removal of the craw after the bird is killed eliminates much of this strong flavor). Most of the birds are about the size of a small chicken, and they are at their best when broiled, roasted, or braised.

Prized by hunters, the wild turkey differs from the domestic variety in that it is extremely lean, requiring constant basting or heavy barding when cooking to keep the dark meat succulent. There is less waste, more solid meat on the wild turkey than on its domestic relative, hence more servings per bird. Smoked wild turkey is acknowledged as one of the finest of all game delicacies. (It is usually served cold, sliced very thin.) And, of course, a roast wild turkey makes a truly authentic Thanksgiving dinner in the tradition of early America.

Early American Roast Turkey

1 turkey (8–10 pounds)
  Salt, pepper
½ pound sausage meat
½ cup finely chopped onion
1 cup finely chopped celery
1 teaspoon salt
¼ teaspoon pepper
¼ teaspoon crushed thyme
¼ teaspoon chervil
¼ cup chopped parsley
1 cup cooked chestnuts, chopped coarsely
8 cups bread crumbs made from day-old bread
8 thick slices bacon
½ cup melted bacon fat

Rinse and dry turkey inside and out. Sprinkle cavity and all surfaces with salt, pepper. Cook sausage until thoroughly done; then add the onion and celery, cooking until transparent. Add salt, pepper, thyme, chervil, and parsley. Add chestnuts, toss in bread crumbs and mix. Fill neck and body with the stuffing. Close cavities with skewers or sew up. Place turkey on rack in roasting pan, breast side up. Pull legs up and tie together with string. Turn wings under. Cover breast with bacon slices and ends of legs with foil.

Soak a piece of cheesecloth in the melted bacon fat and place over bacon-covered breast. Roast breast side up at 325° F. for 20–25 minutes per pound or until done to taste. Baste constantly with fat and pan drippings. Serves 8–10. *Serve with:* giblet gravy, Baked Acorn Squash (page 181), parsnips, corn bread, Whole Fresh Cranberry Sauce (page 183), and ale. This menu makes the traditional Thanksgiving feast.

1 turkey (8–10 pounds)
  Salt, pepper
1 large onion, peeled, quartered
1 whole stalk celery
1 carrot, scraped, quartered
4 slices fat salt pork
1 onion, sliced
2 carrots, sliced
4 sprigs parsley
2 stalks celery, chopped
1 bay leaf
¼ teaspoon crushed, dried thyme
4 cups canned, undiluted consommé
1 tablespoon cornstarch, mixed with 3 tablespoons water

Rinse turkey, drain, and dry thoroughly. Sprinkle inside and out with salt, pepper. Place the onion, celery stalk, and carrot in the cavity. Tie legs together with string and fold wings under. Cover breast with the fat salt pork. Place in a covered roasting pan and roast at 400° F., uncovered, until browned. Skim fat from pan and add the sliced onion, carrots, parsley, celery, bay leaf, thyme, and consommé. Cover pan tightly and cook on top of stove over medium heat or in oven at 350° F. until tender (about 2 hours). Baste fre-quently with pan juices. When done, transfer bird to heated platter and keep warm. Strain the pan juices and add the cornstarch mixture, stirring over medium heat until sauce is thickened. Serve gravy on side. Serves 8–10.

Serve with: baked sweet potatoes or yams, Stewed Apples (page 183), or Whole Fresh Cranberry Sauce (page 183), Onions Curaçao (page 176), hot corn bread.

Turkey en Cocotte

1 turkey (about 8 pounds)
Salt, pepper
½ pound finely ground veal
½ pound finely ground pork
1 large onion, chopped, sautéed in butter or margarine
½ pound mushrooms, sliced, sautéed in butter or margarine
4–5 slices fat salt pork
1½ cups stock or bouillon
1½ cups dry white wine
1 clove garlic, halved
¼ teaspoon dried thyme
1 small bay leaf
1 tablespoon chopped parsley
2 whole cloves
¼ teaspoon dried basil
2 large onions, peeled, sliced
1 parsnip, scraped, sliced
Flour

Rinse and dry turkey. Sprinkle inside and out with salt, pepper. Mix together the veal, pork, onion, and mushrooms, seasoning well with salt, pepper. Spoon into turkey cavity and close with skewers or sew up. Tie legs together and fold wings under. Cover breast with the salt pork slices.

Place turkey in an iron cocotte or pot with a tight lid. Add the bouillon, wine, and all remaining ingredients except flour. Cover and cook gently over low heat until turkey is tender (2–3 hours). Transfer turkey to heated platter and keep warm. Skim fat from pan juices. Strain juices and thicken with flour. Serve gravy in bowl on side. Serves 8.
Serve with: Whole Fresh Cranberry Sauce (page 183), Baked Acorn Squash (page 181), creamed white onions, corn bread.

1 turkey (8–10 pounds), with giblets reserved
  Salt, pepper
  Fat salt pork slices to cover breast
2 sticks butter or margarine
2 medium onions, chopped fine
¾ pound sausage meat
  Turkey giblets, sautéed in butter or margarine, chopped
    fine
6 cups corn bread crumbs
½ teaspoon dried thyme
½ teaspoon dried sage
¼ teaspoon dried marjoram
3 tablespoons chopped fresh parsley
½ cup sweet white wine (or more as needed)
  Salt, pepper to taste
  Flour

Rinse and dry turkey inside and out. Sprinkle cavity and skin with salt, pepper. Cover breast with fat salt pork slices. Set aside, and make dressing: Melt butter and sauté onions until translucent, but do not brown. Remove onions to mixing bowl and cook sausage in the butter until brown and done. Turn into mixing bowl with the onions. Add the chopped giblets, corn-bread crumbs, thyme, sage, marjoram, and parsley. Mix thoroughly. Add enough of the white wine to make a moist dressing. Add salt, pepper to taste. Fill neck and cavity with stuffing and close both with skewers or sew up. Tie legs together and fold back wings. Place turkey on rack in roasting pan and roast in oven at 350° F. for 20 minutes per pound or until done. Baste frequently with drippings to keep bird moist. Transfer to heated platter and keep warm. Skim fat from pan drippings and make gravy by thickening drippings with flour. Strain, reheat, and serve on side with turkey. Serves 8–10.

Serve with: Whole Fresh Cranberry Sauce (page 183).

Note: Madeira or port wine may be substituted for the white wine, and some of the wine may be added to the gravy after straining it.

Pheasant with Apricots

2 young pheasants (about 2 pounds each)
  Salt, pepper
6 slices fat bacon
1 stick butter or margarine
2 tablespoons flour, mixed wth 3 tablespoons water
1 cup light cream, slightly warmed
  Salt, pepper
1 large can apricots
2 tablespoons gin, warmed
1 tablespoon apricot brandy (optional)
¼ cup chopped almonds

Sprinkle pheasants inside and out with salt and pepper. Wrap three slices of bacon around each bird and secure with toothpicks or thread. Melt butter and pour into a roasting pan. Place birds in pan, breast sides up, and roast at 375° F. for 45 minutes or until tender and done (when fork-tested, juices should run clear). Remove birds to serving platter. Remove bacon and cut birds in serving pieces. Set aside and keep warm. Skim excess fat from pan juices and place over medium heat. Stir in flour mixture and cook, stirring, until thick and smooth. Slowly add the cream, stirring constantly, and continue to heat until lightly thickened. Add salt and pepper to taste. Set aside, keeping sauce warm while apricots are heated through in their juice. Drain and arrange around platter of pheasant portions. Pour the warmed gin over the pheasant and ignite. When flames die, pour heated sauce over pheasant. Sprinkle apricots with brandy, if desired, and with the chopped almonds. Serves 4–6.

Serve with: Braised Endive (page 179).

Pheasant, Chinese Style

2 young pheasants (about 2½ pounds each)
4 slices fat salt pork
½ cup soy sauce
½ cup peanut oil
½ cup sherry
1 teaspoon powdered ginger
2 cloves garlic, minced fine

Rinse and dry pheasants. Place 2 slices of the fat salt pork in each cavity. Tie legs together with string and fold wings back. Place and center on electric spit. Mix all remaining ingredients in a screw-top jar, tighten lid in place, and shake vigorously. Spit-roast birds over hot coals or high heat, basting constantly with the mixture. Catch drippings under birds and use also for constant basting. Roast till deep brown, tender, and done—about 45–55 minutes, depending on size of birds. Serves 4.

Serve with: bed of white or wild rice with a dozen preserved kumquats circling platter as garnish.

Pheasant à l'Orange

3 small young pheasants (about 2 pounds each), dressed, halved lengthwise
1 small lemon, halved
  Salt, pepper
1 stick butter or margarine
3 medium navel oranges
1 cup white raisins
1 tablespoon curaçao
½ cup sweet white wine
1 cup chicken stock or broth

Wipe pheasant halves dry with paper towels. Rub all surfaces with the cut halves of lemon. Sprinkle lightly with salt, pepper. Place in roasting pan, breast sides up, and coat liberally with the butter. Grate enough lemon peel for 2 level teaspoons and sprinkle over birds. Juice the oranges (reserve shells), strain and add to pan. Add all remaining ingredients and bake at 350° F. for 45 minutes, basting frequently to keep surfaces moist. Serve with the pan mixture poured over. Serves 6.

Serve with: **Pecan-Rice Orange Cups (page 181).**

Pheasant in Champagne

2 2-pound pheasants, dressed, cut in serving pieces
1 bottle champagne
2 medium onions, chopped fine
2 medium carrots, sliced thin
1 large stalk celery (top included), sliced thin
1 tablespoon minced fresh parsley
½ teaspoon salt
¼ teaspoon pepper
1 stick butter or margarine
1 jigger cognac, heated
½ pint cream
1 teaspoon cornstarch mixed with 1 tablespoon water

Combine half the champagne with onions, carrot, celery, parsley, salt, pepper. Use to marinate pheasant for 24 hours. Drain, reserving marinade. Dry pieces and sauté in butter in a deep skillet until golden. Add marinade, cover and simmer for 20–30 minutes or until tender. Pour cognac over; ignite. When flames die, add remaining champagne and simmer for 30 minutes, uncovered. Transfer pheasant to heated platter. Stir in cream, bring to boil, but do not boil. Add cornstarch mixture and simmer, stirring, until thickened. Pour over pheasant. Serves 4.
Serve with: fried bread triangles and watercress garnish.

Pheasant in Sour Cream

2 small pheasants (about 2 pounds each)
1½ sticks butter or margarine
 Paprika
 Salt
8 strips bacon
6 whole small onions, peeled
1 pint sour cream

Wipe pheasants inside and out. Coat all surfaces with butter and sprinkle with paprika and salt. Place breasts up in a deep ovenproof casserole. Cover with the bacon slices and tuck the onions around the birds. Place in preheated 400° F. oven and roast until birds begin to brown (about 45 minutes). Add additional butter to casserole to keep bottom moist. Pour sour cream over the birds and continue roasting for another 10 minutes, spooning the cream over them from time to time. Serves 4.
Serve with: buttered noodles or wild rice.

Salmi of Pheasant

2 pheasants (about 2 pounds each)
2 tablespoons butter or margarine
   Salt, pepper
8 strips bacon
1 stick butter or margarine
1 large onion, coarsely chopped
1 clove garlic, minced fine
2 medium carrots, sliced thin
1 tablespoon instant flour
1 cup red wine
1 cup bouillon or chicken stock
   Pinch each thyme, chervil
12 medium mushrooms, sliced and lightly sautéed in butter or
    margarine
6 slices buttered toast, crusts trimmed
1 small can pâté (goose or chicken liver), optional

Place a tablespoon of butter in the cavity of each bird. Sprinkle with salt, pepper on all surfaces. Cover breasts with bacon and place, breast sides up, on rack in a roasting pan. Roast in preheated 350° F. oven for 45 minutes or until birds are crisp and done to taste. Meanwhile, prepare sauce: In a large skillet melt the stick of butter and sauté onion, garlic, and carrots until tender and golden. Sprinkle in the flour, stirring over medium heat. Add the wine and bouillon and continue stirring until slightly thickened. Add thyme, chervil, and the mushrooms. Simmer over very low heat. Remove bacon from birds when done and cut birds into serving pieces. Spread toast with the pâté and place on heated platter. Arrange birds on toast and pour the hot sauce over all. Serves 4.

Serve with: Chestnut Purée (page 173) and currant jelly or Wild Beach Plum Jelly (page 184).

Roast Pheasant Flambé

1 large pheasant (about 3 pounds)
1 pheasant liver
1/4 pound pork sausage meat
1 teaspoon butter
8 medium-size mushrooms, chopped
2 large sprigs parsley, chopped
1 egg, lightly beaten
1/4 teaspoon freshly ground black pepper
3 slices white bread soaked in 1/4 cup milk
1/4 cup brandy
4 slices bacon

Lightly brown the liver and sausage meat in the butter. Add the mushrooms and parsley, blending and stirring over medium heat for 2–3 minutes. Transfer to mixing bowl, cool, and add the beaten egg and pepper. Add bread to mixture. Blend well and fill cavity of pheasant loosely. Close cavity. Place bird on rack in roasting pan and pour half of brandy over it. Ignite. When flame dies, cover breast with bacon strips and roast in preheated 375° F. oven for 40 minutes or until done. Remove bacon strips and transfer bird to heated platter. Pour remaining brandy, heated, over bird. Ignite at table. Serves 2–4.
Serve with: Braised Endive (page 179).

Clay Pot Roast Pheasant

2 pheasants (about 2 pounds each)
 Sherry Marinade (page 154)
8 strips fatty bacon

Place birds in a deep crock or ceramic bowl and pour the marinade over them. Refrigerate or place in a cool spot for 12–14 hours, turning the birds 4–5 times so that all surfaces are coated with the marinade. Drain birds (reserve marinade) and cover each breast with 4 strips of bacon. Place, breast sides up, in an unglazed clay pot with snug lid, pour half of the marinade around the birds, and roast, covered, in a 350° F. oven until tender (about 1½ hours). Add additional marinade as needed to keep birds moist. Serves 4.
Serve with: Braised Celery (page 179) and Wild Rice Casserole (page 170).

Pheasant with Port

1 large pheasant (about 2½–3 pounds)
  Salt, pepper
12 crushed coriander seeds
½ stick butter, melted
1 cup good port, warmed
2 cups Basic Brown Sauce (page 157), heated, reduced to 1 cup
1 cup heavy cream, slightly warmed
  Watercress for garnish

Rub salt, pepper, and crushed coriander on surfaces and in cavity of bird. Place, breast side up, in roasting pan and brush with melted butter. Pour remaining butter around bird. Roast at 350° F. for 45 minutes to 1 hour, basting frequently with the butter, until bird is golden brown and done (when fork-tested, juices run clear). Remove from oven and cut in serving portions. Keep warm on heated platter. Skim excess fat from pan and add the port. Stir over medium heat. Add the reduced brown sauce, stirring till well-blended. Slowly stir in the warmed cream, reduce heat, and continue to stir until sauce thickens. Pour over the pheasant. Garnish with watercress. Serves 3–4.
Serve with: wild rice or Rice Pilaf (page 171).

Simple Roast Pheasant

1 young pheasant (2 to 3 pounds)
  Salt, pepper
1 bay leaf
2–3 celery stalk tops
1 thick slice lemon
4 slices fatty bacon
1 stick butter or margarine, melted
1 cup stock or strong chicken broth
1 large onion, sliced
¼ pound whole fresh button mushrooms
  Flour or cornstarch

Rinse and dry pheasant. Sprinkle inside and out with salt, pepper. Place bay leaf, celery leaves, and lemon slice in cavity. Turn wings under and tie legs together with string. Lay bacon slices over breast and cover with several layers of cheesecloth soaked in the melted butter. Put bird on rack in roasting pan, breast side up. Pour in the stock and add onion slices and mushrooms. Roast, basting often with the pan drippings, at 350° F. for 30 minutes per pound or until bird is tender and done. Remove cheesecloth, bacon, and string. Skim the pan drippings and thicken with flour or cornstarch to make gravy. Serves 2–4.
Serve with: Savory Wild Rice with Raisins (page 170).

Pheasant Pie

1 pheasant (2 to 3 pounds)
1 stalk celery
1 bay leaf
6 peppercorns
1 tablespoon salt
1 stick butter or margarine
5 tablespoons flour
1 cup table cream or half-and-half
   Freshly ground black pepper
   Pinch of salt
24 small whole white onions, parboiled
¼ pound fresh mushrooms, sliced
2 cups cooked fresh peas or 1 package frozen peas, thawed
1 unbaked pie crust circle to cover casserole

Rinse pheasant and place in large pot with water to cover. Add the celery, bay leaf, peppercorns, and salt. Cover and simmer over low heat until bird is tender and meat may easily be removed from bones (about 1–2 hours). Remove meat from bones and set aside. Strain 1 pint of the liquid and reserve. Melt butter in a saucepan and blend in the flour. Gradually add the reserved liquid, stirring. Add the cream or half-and-half, and salt and pepper. Cook over medium heat, stirring constantly, until thickened. Place pheasant pieces in a large (2-quart) casserole and add the onions, mushrooms, and peas. Pour sauce over all, leaving 1 inch or more space at top. Place pastry over casserole, turning edges under and pressing with fingers or fork. Bake at 450 ° F. until crust is golden brown (about 15–20 minutes). Serves 4.
Serve with: crisp mixed green salad.

Pheasant in Cream

2 young pheasants (2–2½ pounds each)
4 sprigs fresh parsley
2 juniper berries (optional)
2 pinches dried thyme
1 stick butter or margarine
   Salt, pepper
1 cup consommé
¼ cup sherry
1 tablespoon butter or margarine
1 tablespoon flour
1 pint cream, warmed
¼ teaspoon nutmeg
4 slices crisp buttered toast, crusts trimmed

Rinse and dry birds inside and out. In each cavity place 2 sprigs parsley, 1 juniper berry, and a pinch of thyme. Melt butter in a flameproof casserole. Brown birds in butter. Sprinkle with salt, pepper. Add consommé and sherry. Lower heat, cover, and simmer until tender (about 1 hour). Melt the tablespoon of butter in a saucepan. Blend in flour and slowly add cream. Add nutmeg and stir until thickened. Place birds on and pour sauce over all. Serves 4.
Serve with: watercress salad, Braised Endive (page 179).

Stuffed Breast of Pheasant

4 whole pheasant breasts, boned
1 stick butter or margarine
¾ cup sliced mushrooms
1 teaspoon minced onion
1 cup coarse bread crumbs
½ teaspoon dried chervil
   Salt, pepper
1 tablespoon cream
4 slices bacon
½ cup stock or strong chicken broth
1 can cream of mushroom soup
½ can milk
1 tablespoon sherry

Melt butter in a heavy skillet. Sauté mushrooms for 5 minutes together with the onion. Add bread crumbs and stir over medium heat until lightly browned. Add the chervil, salt and pepper to taste, and the tablespoon of cream. Dry the breasts. Spread with stuffing, fold, wrap each in a bacon slice, and secure. Place in skillet and pour in stock. Cover and simmer for 20 minutes or until tender. Remove bacon, transfer to heated platter. Heat soup and milk together. Stir in sherry. Pour over breasts. Serves 4.
Serve with: Braised Endive (page 179).

Quail Chasseur

8 quail
  Salt, pepper
  Flour
1½ sticks butter or margarine
  3 cups consommé (canned, undiluted)
¼ teaspoon dried thyme
  1 bay leaf
¾ cup dry white wine

Rinse and dry quail. Sprinkle inside and out with the salt, pepper, and flour. Melt butter in large iron skillet and brown quail in it on all sides over medium heat. Add consommé, thyme, bay leaf, and wine. Cover tightly and simmer over low heat for 30 minutes or until birds are tender. Serve with pan juices poured over. Serves 4.
Serve with: Wild Beach Plum Jelly (page 184) and wild rice.

Baked Quail in Port

6 whole plump quail
  Pepper, salt
6 slices bacon
3 whole oranges, sliced thin
3 medium onions, sliced thin
3 large stalks celery, cut in ½-inch rounds
2 cups chicken stock or consommé
1 cup port

Sprinkle quail inside and out with pepper, salt. Wrap and secure a slice of bacon around each bird, covering legs to hold close to body. Place together in a roasting pan and add all remaining ingredients. Roast in preheated 375° F. oven for 30 minutes or until tender. Remove bacon, strain gravy, and serve with gravy poured over. Serves 3–4.
Serve with: wild rice and Braised Celery (page 179).

Quail with Oysters

 6 plump quail, dressed and split down the back
   Salt, pepper
1½ dozen large oysters with their liquor
 ½ stick butter or margarine

Wipe, dry, and chill birds overnight in refrigerator. Sprinkle inside and out with salt, pepper. Drain oysters and reserve the liquor. Place 3 large oysters in each quail and tie together (or skewer) with wings and legs close to body. Arrange close together in a baking casserole and pour oyster liquor over them. Dot birds liberally with butter, cover casserole snugly, and roast at 350° F for 1 hour or until birds are tender and juices run clear. Serve in the casserole with some of the resulting gravy spooned over each portion. Serves 3–4.
Serve with: wild rice.

Quail Casserole

 8 quail
   Salt, pepper
 8 slices thick, fatty bacon
 1 crushed bay leaf
 ¼ teaspon nutmeg
 ¼ teaspoon thyme
 1 medium onion, chopped fine
 1 large carrot, peeled, chopped fine
16 tiny whole white onions, peeled
24 tiny button mushrooms
 1 tablespoon chopped chives
 1 tablespoon chopped fresh parsley
 1 cup dry white wine
 1 cup chicken bouillon
 2 cups fresh peas or thawed frozen peas
 2 cups hot cooked wild rice

Rinse quail in cold water and dry thoroughly inside and out. Sprinkle inside with salt, pepper. Place half a slice of bacon inside each cavity. Sprinkle outside with salt, pepper, bay leaf, nutmeg, and thyme. Cover breasts with remaining halves of bacon slices. Place in bottom of ovenproof casserole the chopped and whole onions, carrot, mushrooms, chives, and parsley. Place birds on this. Pour in from the side the wine and bouillon. Add the peas. Cover casserole tightly and place in preheated 350° F. oven. Bake for 35 minutes and check for doneness. Serve directly from the casserole over the wild rice. Serves 4.

Serve with: crisp green salad, hot French bread, and Braised Endive (page 179) or Braised Celery (page 179).

Quail Flambé

4 quail
½ lemon
   Salt, pepper
   Flour
½ stick butter or margarine
¼ cup cognac, warmed

Rinse and dry the quail. Rub with the lemon on insides and out. Sprinkle with salt, pepper, flour. Melt butter in cast-iron skillet over medium heat and brown birds on all sides in it. Transfer skillet with birds to preheated 375° F. oven and roast, basting frequently, for 20 minutes or until birds are tender and done. When fork-tested between leg and breast, juice should run clear. Transfer birds to heated platter. Pour cognac over them and ignite. When flame dies, pour pan juices over birds and serve at once. Serves 2.

Serve with: wild rice, Braised Celery (page 179), and watercress salad.

Broiled Quail

8 quail
8 crab apples, cored, seeded
8 small onions, peeled
1½ cups melted butter or margarine
   Salt, pepper

Rinse quail in cold water and dry thoroughly. Place an apple and an onion in each cavity. Brush birds liberally with melted butter and sprinkle with salt and pepper. Broil, turning and basting with butter, until tender and crisply brown—about 30 minutes. Serves 4.
Serve with: Currant Jelly Sauce (page 161) and wild rice.

Quail-in-the-Ashes

8 quail
2 cups cooked wild rice
   Salt, pepper
   Fresh thyme (optional)
8 thin slices fat salt pork

Rinse and dry the quail. Fill cavities with wild rice and close with small skewers. Sprinkle with salt, pepper. Wrap each in a slice of fat salt pork, then wrap securely in heavy aluminum foil. Enclose a sprig of thyme in each packet, if desired. Bury packets in hot charcoal ashes in a barbecue pit, fireplace, or outdoor campfire. Let roast for 35 minutes and check for tenderness. Cook 10 minutes more, or as needed. Be sure to keep birds piled with hot ashes throughout cooking. Serves 4.
Serve with: Currant Jelly Sauce (page 161).

Quail with Cherries

8 quail
1 stick butter or margarine
1 cup canned consommé, undiluted
½ cup port or Madeira wine
1 tablespoon grated lemon rind
¼ cup tart cherry jelly
1 cup pitted Bing cherries (canned or fresh)
1 tablespoon lemon juice
  Salt, pepper

Melt butter in a heavy skillet and brown birds evenly on all surfaces. Cover and bake in a 375° F. oven for 30 minutes. Transfer to a heated serving plate. Skim pan juices and add the consommé, wine, and lemon rind. Place over medium heat and simmer for about 10 minutes, stirring once or twice. Add the jelly, drained cherries, and lemon juice. Simmer 5 minutes longer; season with salt and pepper. Pour over the quail. Serves 4.
Serve with: wild rice and mixed green salad.
Note: When using fresh cherries, simmer 10 minutes more.

Quail in Trenchers

4 quail
  Salt, pepper
  Flour
½ stick butter or margarine
½ cup chicken stock or bouillon
12 mushrooms, sliced
2 tablespoons finely chopped parsley
4 trenchers (halved large hard rolls, centers scooped out, buttered and toasted)

Rinse quail in cold water and dry thoroughly inside and out. Squinkle cavities and skin with salt, pepper, and flour. Melt butter in large skillet and brown quail on all sides in it. Add stock and mushrooms. Cover tightly and cook over low heat for 10 minutes longer or until tender. Serve in the trenchers with sauce from pan poured over. Serves 4.
Serve with: bowl of chilled raw vegetables—carrots, radishes, scallions, cauliflower, green beans, and salt.
Note: This is a good, quick luncheon dish. Recipe may be halved or doubled.

Quail with Green Grapes

4 quail
  Salt, pepper
  Flour
½ stick butter or margarine
½ cup water
½ cup seedless green grapes
1 tablespoon white wine
4 pieces bread, crusts trimmed, fried crisp in butter or margarine

Rinse and dry quail. Sprinkle inside and out with salt, pepper, and flour. Melt butter in large skillet and brown quail on all sides in it. Add water, cover tightly, and simmer for 15 minutes or until tender. Add grapes. Cook 3 minutes longer. Stir in the wine. Serve on fried toast slices with pan juices poured over and a few grapes on each plate. Serves 2.
Serve with: Chestnut Purée (page 173).
Note: Recipe may be doubled or tripled for more servings.

Partridge in Vine Leaves

4 plump partridges
  Juice of 1 lemon
  Salt, pepper
½ teaspoon powdered cloves
½ teaspoon powdered ginger
8 slices fatty bacon
12 grape leaves
½ cup dry red wine
6 medium mushrooms, chopped, sautéed in butter
1 tablespoon red currant jelly
3 tablespoons cream
½ cup bread crumbs lightly browned in ¼ stick butter

Brush birds with lemon juice and sprinkle lightly with the salt, pepper, cloves, and ginger. Wrap and cover each in 2 slices of bacon and place in a roasting pan. Cover with the grape leaves and pour in the wine. Roast for 20 minutes in a preheated 400° F. oven. Remove leaves and bacon. Spoon pan drippings over birds and turn up oven to 475° for 5–10 minutes or until birds are crisp-brown. Transfer to heated platter; keep warm. Heat pan juices and stir in mushrooms, jelly, and cream, blending thoroughly. Sprinkle birds with the crumbs and serve sauce on side. Serves 4.
Serve with: Brussels Sprouts with Grapes (page 178).

Partridge with Cabbage

2 plump partridges, split in halves
   Salt, pepper
8 slices bacon, diced
1 firm head of savoy cabbage (about 1 pound)
2 large carrots, cut in thin rounds
1 large turnip, diced
¼ teaspoon thyme
   Pinch nutmeg
½ teaspoon caraway seeds
2 cups chicken stock, broth, or consommé

Wipe partridges and lightly season with salt, pepper. Cook bacon in large skillet until crisp. Remove and reserve bacon. Brown partridge in the bacon fat. Trim, wash, and pull cabbage leaves apart. Line an ovenproof casserole (with tight-fitting lid) with outer leaves. Arrange partridges on bottom, add carrots and turnip. Sprinkle with the seasonings. Add bacon and cover with 3–4 layers of cabbage leaves. Add stock. Cover casserole and place in 325° F. oven for 1½ hours or until birds are tender. Serves 2–4.
Serve with: fluffy mashed potatoes.

Partridge in White Wine

3 large partridges cut in serving pieces (quartered)
½ stick butter or margarine
   Salt, pepper
2 cups dry white wine
1 clove garlic, minced
¼ teaspoon thyme
½ teaspoon basil
½ teaspoon marjoram
1 tablespoon chopped fresh parsley
1 tablespoon instant flour

Wipe bird pieces dry. Melt butter in a heatproof casserole over medium heat. Brown the pieces on all sides and sprinkle with salt, pepper. Pour wine over them and add all remaining ingredients except flour. Bring to boil, lower heat, and simmer, covered tightly, until tender and done. Sprinkle instant flour over liquid, stir over medium heat till slightly thickened. Serve in the casserole. Serves 4.
Serve with: Baked Acorn Squash (page 181) and green salad.

Partridge in Cream

3 partridges, quartered
Salt, pepper
½ stick butter or margarine
2½ cups stock or undiluted canned consommé
1 tablespoon minced fresh parsley
18 button mushrooms
1 teaspoon instant minced onion
1 tablespoon instant flour
½ pint cream
Parsley sprigs

Wipe partridge quarters dry. Sprinkle with salt, pepper. Melt butter in a cocotte or iron pot and brown the pieces on all sides. Pour in the stock or consommé. Add the parsley, mushrooms, and minced onion. Simmer, covered, over low heat for about 1 hour or until tender and done. Transfer partridges to heated serving platter and keep warm. Turn up heat and cook remaining liquid until about 1 cup remains. Sprinkle flour over liquid, stir, cooking over low heat until slightly thickened. Slowly add cream, stirring, until sauce is consistency of medium-thick gravy. Pour over partridge. Garnish with parsley sprigs. Serves 4.
Serve with: Pecan-Rice Orange Cups (page 181).

Casserole of Partridge

4 small plump partridges
8 juniper berries (optional)
½ stick butter or margarine
Salt, pepper
2 medium carrots, diced
2 medium onions, chopped fine
2 stalks celery, chopped fine
4 slices cold boiled ham, cut in ¼-inch strips
¼ pound mushrooms, sliced
1 tablespoon minced parsley
¼ teaspoon dried thyme
2 cups stock or undiluted canned consommé
2 tablespoons brandy

Rinse and dry birds inside and out. Put 2 juniper berries in each cavity. Melt butter in a heatproof casserole and brown birds on all sides over medium heat. Sprinkle with salt, pepper. Remove birds and set aside. Put all remaining ingredients in casserole and place birds, breast sides down, on top. Cover tightly and place casserole in preheated 400° F. oven for 40 minutes or until birds are tender (time will vary with size of birds). Serve birds from casserole with the vegetables and juices around them. Serves 4.

Roast Stuffed Partridge

2 large partridges
  Salt, pepper
4 slices fatty bacon
1½ cups cooked wild rice, or half wild and half brown rice
8 medium-size mushrooms, chopped, sautéed in butter
1½ cups stock or good bouillon

Rinse and dry partridge inside and out. Sprinkle with salt, pepper. Cover breasts with the bacon slices. Mix rice and mushrooms together and spoon half of the mixture into cavity of each bird. Close cavities with small skewers. Place birds in roasting pan. Pour in the stock and roast birds at 400° F. for 25–30 minutes or until tender and done. Serves 2. *Serve with:* wild rice and tart currant or Wild Beach Plum Jelly (page 184) on the side.

Savory Roast Partridge

4 partridges
1 lemon, halved
  Salt
1 teaspoon thyme
4 pieces fat salt pork, ¼ inch thick
4 small stalks celery
4 sprigs parsley
2 bay leaves
4 small white onions, peeled, halved
4 slices bread, crisp-fried in butter

Rinse and dry birds inside and out. Rub all over with the cut halves of lemon and squeeze a little lemon juice into each cavity. Sprinkle birds with salt and the thyme. Cover breasts with the pieces of salt pork. Insert in each cavity 1 stalk celery, 1 sprig parsley, ½ bay leaf, and 1 onion. Tie salt pork in place with string. Place birds, breast sides up, on rack in roasting pan and roast at 400° F. for 30–35 minutes or until tender. Remove string and salt pork about 5 minutes before birds are done for a brown, crisp skin. Remove parsley, celery, onion, and bay leaf from each cavity. Serve on crisp-fried toast. Skim fat from pan drippings and pour remaining juices over birds. Serves 4. *Serve with:* Brussels Sprouts with Grapes (page 178).

Partridge with Cabbage and Chestnuts

4 partridges
  Salt, pepper
  Juice of 1 lemon
½ stick butter or margarine
4 slices bacon
1 medium-size red or white cabbage
1 tablespoon sugar
1 cup apple cider
1 cup cooked chestnuts, shelled, peeled

Rinse and dry birds thoroughly. Sprinkle inside and out with lemon juice, salt, pepper. Melt butter in large skillet and brown birds slowly. Remove birds, wrap each in bacon, and secure with picks or string. Shred the cabbage coarsely and add it to the skillet in which birds have been browned. Sprinkle with sugar and pour in the cider. Lay birds, breast sides down, on top. Cover tightly and simmer slowly over low heat for 1 hour or until birds are tender. Turn birds breast sides up during last 10 minutes of cooking and add the chestnuts. Serve birds on the bed of stewed cabbage. Serves 4.
Serve with: hot corn muffins.

Oven-Stewed Grouse

2 large grouse, quartered
  Salt, pepper
½ stick butter or margarine
2 medium onions, sliced thin
2 stalks celery (tops included), cut in ½-inch rounds
2 large carrots, peeled, cut in ¼-inch rounds
20 medium mushrooms, sliced
¼ teaspoon sage
½ dozen pork sausages
2 cups chicken stock or broth

Sprinkle bird parts with salt, pepper. Melt butter in large skillet and brown birds over medium heat. In a covered roasting pan, make a layer of the onions, celery, carrots, and mushrooms. Sprinkle on the sage. Place sausages in a ring around outer edge of layered vegetables. Place grouse quarters in center. Pour over the stock and cover. Bake in preheated 325° F. oven for 1½–2 hours until meat nearly falls from bones. Serve in casserole with vegetables and sausage as originally arranged. Serves 4.
Serve with: Stewed Apples (page 183) and a crisp green salad.

Grouse à l'Orange

4 small grouse
  Salt, pepper
4 navel orange slices, peels trimmed
4 slices fatty bacon
1 stick butter or margarine, melted
2 tablespoons grated orange peel
2 tablespoons fresh orange juice
1 teaspoon lemon juice
1 tablespoon chopped fresh parsley

Rinse and dry birds inside and out and sprinkle with salt, pepper. Cover each breast with an orange slice, top it with a bacon slice and secure with string. Place, breast sides up, in roasting pan. Roast at 350° F. for 15 minutes or until tender and done to taste. Baste frequently with a mixture of the butter, orange peel, and orange and lemon juices. Remove strings when done, leaving orange slices in place. Place on heated serving platter and sprinkle with the chopped parsley. Strain pan juices and serve as is on side to pour over. Serves 4.
Serve with: fluffy mashed sweet potatoes or baked yams.

Braised Grouse

  2 breasts of grouse
  1 stick butter or margarine
    Salt, pepper
1½ cups stock or good bouillon
  1 small carrot, sliced thin
  1 small onion, sliced thin
  1 stalk celery, chopped
  1 teaspoon chopped fresh parsley
  ½ bay leaf
  2 tablespoons flour
  ¾ cup canned plum tomatoes, drained
  1 teaspoon lemon juice
  ½ cup sautéed sliced mushrooms

Melt ½ stick of butter in heavy iron skillet. Sauté grouse breasts until brown. Sprinkle with salt, pepper. Add stock, carrot, onion, celery, parsley, and bay leaf. Simmer, covered, over low heat until tender. Remove breasts to heated serving dish and keep warm. Strain skillet liquids. Melt remaining butter and blend with the flour. Add strained liquid, stirring till thickened. Add tomatoes. Sprinkle lemon juice over sauce and add mushrooms. Simmer for 5 minutes. Pour over grouse. Serves 2.
Serve with: wild, brown, or white rice.

Grouse Amandine

4 small grouse
Salt, pepper
4 slices fatty bacon
1 stick butter or margarine, melted
½ cup blanched almonds, slivered
1 teaspoon lemon juice
4 slices bread, crusts trimmed, fried crisp in butter or
    margarine
Watercress for garnish

Rinse and dry grouse thoroughly. Sprinkle inside and out with salt, pepper. Cover breasts with the bacon and tie in place with string. Place birds, breast sides up, in a roasting pan. Roast at 350° F. for 15 minutes or until tender and done, basting frequently with half of the melted butter and the pan drippings. Meanwhile, add the almonds and lemon juice to remaining butter and heat. Place grouse, strings and bacon removed, on fried bread slices. Pour almond-butter sauce over all. Garnish with watercress. Serves 4.

Serve with: fresh asparagus or broccoli with melted butter.

Broiled Grouse

2 grouse, split down backs
4 cups red wine
6 whole cloves
1 medium onion, sliced
1 bay leaf
1 teaspoon dried sage
Flour
Salt, pepper
Melted butter or margarine
4 slices buttered toast, cut into points

Place grouse in bowl; cover with wine. Add the cloves, onion, bay leaf, and sage. Refrigerate overnight, turning the grouse several times. Drain grouse and pat dry, reserving marinade. Sprinkle with flour and season with salt, pepper. Place on broiling rack, skin sides down, and broil, turning once, for about 15 minutes or until done. Brush with melted butter several times to keep flesh moist. When done, transfer to heated serving platter and keep warm. Thicken pan juices with flour and add, stirring, 1 cup of the strained marinade. Heat till thickened, stirring. Serve on side with the grouse. Arrange toast points around grouse platter. Serves 2–4.

Serve with: Baked Stuffed Mushrooms (page 182).

Grouse in Madeira

2 large grouse, cut in 8 serving pieces or quartered
4 cups Madeira wine
3 small onions, halved, stuck with 6 whole cloves
1 bay leaf
1 teaspoon crushed dried rosemary
½ cup flour
   Salt, pepper
½ stick butter or margarine

Place grouse pieces in deep ceramic or glass bowl and cover with marinade made of the wine, onions, bay leaf, rosemary. Refrigerate for two or three days, turning the pieces occasionally so that all surfaces soak in the marinade. Drain pieces and wipe dry. Reserve the marinade. Dust with flour, salt, and pepper. Melt butter in a heatproof casserole and brown pieces on all sides. Add the marinade, cover tightly, and bake at 300° F. for about 45 minutes or until tender. Pour off marinade, strain, heat, and thicken with flour. Pour back in casserole. Serves 4.
Serve with: Savory Wild Rice with Raisins (page 170).

Woodcock with Oysters

4 woodcocks, dressed, dried, sprinkled with salt, pepper
24 raw oysters, poached in their juice (juice reserved)
1 cup very thick white sauce made with the oyster liquor and
   cream
4 slices bacon
4 slices bread, crisp-fried in butter
   Anchovy paste
2 tablespoons brandy
2 tablespoons melted butter
2 lemons cut in quarters

Combine oysters with the thick white sauce. Divide and fill cavities of birds, allowing 6 oysters for each. Wrap birds with bacon; secure. Bake at 350° F. until golden (about 20 minutes). Spread the anchovy paste on the fried bread slices. Place birds on tops of these. Dilute juices in roasting pan with the brandy and stir in butter. Heat and pour over birds. Serve with the lemon wedges. Serves 4.
Serve with: endive or chicory salad with vinegar-oil dressing.

Boned Woodcock, Stuffed

4 woodcocks, dressed, boned (reserve bones)
4 cooked woodcock livers, gizzards, hearts (sautéed in butter or
    margarine or cooked in bouillon)
    Salt, pepper
½ teaspoon poultry seasoning
4 tablespoons cognac, warmed
¼ cup fine bread crumbs
1 raw egg yolk
4 slices bacon
4 1 stick butter or margarine, melted
1 cup stock made from the woodcock bones or 1 cup chicken
    broth
    Watercress

Put livers, gizzards, hearts through meat grinder. Sprinkle with salt, pepper, and poultry seasoning. Add 2 tablespoons cognac and bread crumbs sufficient to make a light, moist stuffing. Mix in the egg yolk and divide stuffing among the four birds. Roll up birds and wrap in slices of bacon. Skewer bacon with wooden picks. Place birds in buttered ovenproof casserole in preheated 450° F. oven for 5 minutes. Reduce heat to 325° and roast 20 minutes more, basting constantly with the melted butter. When birds are nearly done, remove from oven and place over low flame. Warm remaining cognac, ignite, and when flames die, add the stock or broth. Heat through and serve in the casserole. Garnish with watercress. Serves 4.

Serve with: creamed spinach and Rosemary Onions (page 176) or Onions Curaçao (page 176).

Note: Birds may also be stuffed with Olive Wild Rice Stuffing (page 186).

Baked Woodcock

4 woodcocks
1 cup milk
1 cup flour
  Cooking oil
  Salt, pepper
1 pint cream

Wipe and dry birds inside and out. Cut in serving pieces and dip each piece in milk, then in flour. Heat ½ inch of oil in large skillet until a cube of bread turns golden in 1 minute. Brown the pieces on all sides in the oil. Sprinkle with salt, pepper. Transfer to a heatproof casserole and pour cream over all. Bake at 350° F. until tender—about 25 minutes. Serves 4.

Serve with: tossed green salad and crisp shoestring potatoes.

Woodcock with Sour Cream Sauce

4 woodcocks
  Salt, pepper
4 slices bacon
1 stick butter or margarine, melted
  Sour Cream Sauce (pages 162 and 163)
4 slices bread
  Watercress

Wipe dry and sprinkle woodcocks inside and out with salt, pepper. Wrap each bird with bacon and secure with string or a wooden pick. Place in buttered heatproof casserole and roast at 450° F. for 5 minutes. Reduce heat and roast at 325° for 20 minutes more. When bacon is crisp, remove it, and baste birds frequently with some of the melted butter. Meanwhile, prepare sour cream sauce and reserve in bowl to pour over carved birds. Prepare bread by trimming crusts and frying till crisp in remaining melted butter. Serve as a base for birds on individual plates. Garnish casserole with watercress just before bringing to table. Serves 4.

Serve with: wild, brown, or white rice and green beans.

Broiled Woodcock

4 woodcocks
  Salt, pepper
4 slices bacon
1 stick butter or margarine, melted
1 tablespoon finely chopped parsley
4 slices buttered toast, crusts trimmed

Sprinkle woodcocks inside and out with salt and pepper after wiping dry. Wrap each with a slice of bacon and fasten with string or a wooden pick. Place them on broiler pan about 6 inches from heat and broil 8–10 minutes, or until tender. Baste constantly with the melted butter. When done, remove strings or picks and sprinkle with parsley. Serve on the toast slices. Serves 4.
Serve with: Brussel Sprouts with Chestnuts (page 177).

Breast of Woodcock in Cognac

4 woodcocks
4 woodcock livers, chopped
4 thick slices bacon
  Salt, pepper
½ cup cognac, warmed
4 slices buttered toast
  Watercress or parsley sprigs for garnish

Wipe woodcocks inside and out. Wrap each in a slice of bacon and secure bacon with string or wooden pick. Sprinkle with salt, pepper. Roast at 450° F. until bacon is brown—about 12–15 minutes. Remove birds from oven, reserving pan juices. Discard bacon and carve breasts carefully from birds. Chop (or put through coarse meat grinder) the bird carcasses. Place in pan and add 3 tablespoons of the cognac to the pan. Ignite. Add the chopped livers. Skim fat from pan juices and add juices to the carcass mixture. Heat through, but do not boil. Force through fine sieve into another saucepan. Add remaining cognac and heat through again without boiling. Arrange woodcock breasts on buttered toast and pour sauce over them. Garnish with sprigs of watercress or parsley. Serves 4.
Serve with: Chestnut Purée (page 173).

Pigeons with Grapes

4 pigeons, quartered

½ stick butter or margarine

¼ cup finely chopped onion

1 large shallot, peeled, minced

3 tablespoons cognac, warmed

2 cups strong chicken broth or stock

1 cup seedless white grapes

2 tablespoons cognac

1 tablespoon curaçao

¼ cup white raisins soaked in hot water till plump (about 8 hours), optional

1 rounded teaspoon butter or margarine

Salt, pepper

Melt butter in large skillet over high heat. Quickly brown pigeon quarters on both sides. Add onion and shallot. Pour cognac over all and ignite. When flames die, add stock, lower heat, and simmer for 15 minutes or until birds are done. (Partially cover pan while simmering.) Meanwhile, pour cognac and curaçao over grapes; drain raisins, and add. When pigeons are done, transfer to heated platter and keep warm. Pour the liquor from the grapes and raisins into the skillet juices, stir, and cook over medium heat until all is reduced to about 1 cup. Add the grapes and raisins and bring to a boil, stirring, for about 2 minutes. Remove from heat, and gently stir in the butter. Add salt and pepper to taste. Pour over pigeons and serve at once. Serves 4.

Serve with: plain, steamed wild rice or Whipped Potatoes and Turnips (page 174) and Braised Escarole Amandine (page 182).

Note: An additional cup of grapes may be added to recipe, if desired.

Pigeons aux Petits Pois

4 young pigeons, wiped dry, sprinkled with salt, pepper
½ pound bacon, diced
2 teaspoons butter or margarine
2 pounds fresh green peas, shelled
1 tablespoon butter or margarine
1 tablespoon granulated sugar
8 lettuce leaves, torn in pieces or coarsely shredded
8 small white onions
   Flour

Put bacon and 2 teaspoons butter in bottom of ovenproof casserole and place birds on top. Roast in a 350° F. oven for about 25 minutes or until birds are golden brown and tender. Meanwhile prepare peas: Melt the tablespoon of butter in a saucepan, add the peas, sugar, lettuce, and onions. Cover and cook slowly over very low heat for about 20 minutes or until peas are tender, but still crisp. When peas are done, arrange pigeons in center of a heated platter with peas surrounding them. Serves 4.
Serve with: Wild Beach Plum Jelly (page 184) or currant jelly.

Pigeon Casserole

4 young pigeons
4 strips fat bacon
½ stick butter or margarine
1 cup rich stock or strong bouillon
12 small white onions
12 whole button mushrooms
1 cup claret
   Salt, pepper to taste
   Instant flour

Wipe pigeons; wrap with bacon strips and tie in place. Melt butter and sauté birds in the butter until golden brown. Transfer birds to a heatproof casserole, pour stock over, and add all remaining ingredients. Cook, covered, over very low heat for 45–50 minutes. If necessary, thicken the juices with a bit of instant flour. Serve in the casserole. Serves 2–4.
Serve with: wild, brown, or white rice.

Roast Stuffed Pigeons

4 pigeons

4 pigeon livers, sautéed in butter or margarine and coarsely
    chopped

2 cups fresh mushrooms, coarsely chopped

½ cup finely chopped fat salt pork

½ cup fine bread crumbs

    Bouillon

2 eggs, lightly beaten

2 small shallots, minced

1 tablespoon minced fresh parsley

4 slices bacon

¼ cup claret

1 tablespoon cornstarch

2 tablespoons cold water

6 sprigs watercress

Mix together the livers, mushrooms, fat salt pork, and bread crumbs soaked in bouillon and pressed dry. Add the eggs, shallots, and parsley and mix well. Fill pigeon cavities with this mixture and close cavities by sewing or skewering. Place strip of bacon over breast of each bird and arrange in roasting pan. Place in preheated 325° F. oven and roast for 40 minutes or until birds are tender and done to taste. Remove bacon during last 10 minutes to allow birds to brown well.

Baste during this time with the pan juices. Transfer birds to heated platter when done. Keep warm. Skim excess fat from pan juices and add claret, heating and stirring. Thicken with cornstarch mixed with water, if desired. Pour over birds and serve at once with watercress garnish. Serves 4.

Serve with: Braised Endive or Celery (page 179).

Pigeons Italienne

4 pigeons
2 garlic cloves, split
  Freshly ground black pepper
  Flour
1/4 cup olive oil
1 can (8-ounce) tomato sauce
1/2 cup beer
4 medium onions, sliced thin
1/4 teaspoon dried oregano
3 tablespoons chopped fresh parsley

Wipe birds inside and out. Rub surfaces with cut sides of garlic cloves. Sprinkle with pepper and dust with flour. Heat olive oil in large skillet. Add pigeons and brown on all sides. Pour in tomato sauce, beer, onions, and oregano. Bring to boil, lower heat, cover, and cook 30–45 minutes or until tender. Just before serving, stir in parsley. Serves 4.
Serve with: pasta, green salad, crusty Italian bread, and ale or beer.

Brittany Pigeons

6 plump pigeons
1 quart apple cider
1 teaspoon salt
1/2 teaspoon white pepper
1 tablespoon powdered sage
2 tablespoons butter or margarine
1 tablespoon flour
1/2 pound salt pork, minced
6 sprigs parsley
1 sprig fresh thyme
1 large bay leaf
1 dozen blades of chive
3 whole cloves
1 whole clove garlic, peeled
2 dozen button mushrooms
1/4 teaspoon black pepper
2 tablespoons Calvados or applejack, warmed
1 tablespoon minced parsley

Wipe and dry the pigeons. Sprinkle cavities and surfaces with some of the apple cider. Mix together the salt, white pepper, and sage and rub birds inside and out with the mixture. Truss with string or fold legs inside cavities. Set aside and melt butter in a large, heatproof casserole. Blend in flour, stirring until pale gold. Add the salt pork and stir till light brown. Slowly add the cider, stirring until mixture begins to boil. Tie together the parsley, thyme, bay leaf, and chives and add to the boiling mixture. Add cloves, garlic, mushrooms, and pepper. Arrange birds in casserole, breast sides up, and cover tightly. Lower heat and simmer all for 40–45 minutes or until birds are tender. Remove garlic clove and herb bundle and discard. Transfer pigeons to heated platter, arranging them in a ring. Pour heated brandy over birds and ignite. When flames die, pour sauce in center of ring and sprinkle all with parsley. Serves 6.

Serve with: Rosemary Onions (page 176) and watercress garnish.

Note: Recipe may also be used for quail and partridge.

Pigeon with Olives

4 plump pigeons
¼ cup olive oil
1 cup red wine
1 dozen large green, pitted olives
4 leaves dried sage
6 juniper berries
½ teaspoon salt
¼ teaspoon pepper

Wipe and dry pigeons. Heat oil in a large flameproof casserole and brown pigeons on all surfaces. Add all remaining ingredients and transfer casserole to preheated 325° F. oven. Bake for 30–35 minutes or until birds are tender. Serve with sauce right from casserole. Serves 4.

Serve with: Baked Stuffed Mushrooms (page 182) and buttered spinach noodles.

Chili Doves

6 doves
Salt, pepper
6 dried chili peppers
6 thin slices of fat salt pork
6 slices cold boiled ham, diced fine
½ cup chicken stock, heated

Rub doves inside and out with salt, pepper. Place 1 split chili pepper (handle with rubber gloves) in cavity of each bird. Wrap a slice of fat salt pork around each bird and secure. Place birds close together in an ovenproof casserole and add the ham and stock. Cover and place in preheated 350° F. oven for ½ hour. Remove cover and continue to bake for 15 minutes more or until birds are thoroughly browned. Remove pork slices and chili peppers. Serve in casserole with the juices and ham dice. Serves 3–6.
Serve with: hot corn muffins or sticks and grits.
Note: Recipe also works for pigeons.

Breast of Dove with Cointreau

4 boned dove breasts
Flour
Salt, pepper
1 tablespoon butter or margarine
3 tablespoons Cointreau or Triple Sec
1½ cups chicken bouillon or stock
4 thin lemon slices
4 orange slices

Dust dove breasts with flour and sprinkle with salt, pepper. Melt butter in heatproof casserole. Lightly brown breasts on both sides. Pour in heated Cointreau. Ignite. When flames die, add the bouillon and lemon and orange slices. Cover tightly and put in preheated 300° F. oven until tender (about 1 hour). Baste or turn frequently. Serve hot directly from the casserole. Serves 4.
Serve with: new peas with pearl onions and watercress salad.

Doves à la Provençale

4 plump doves
8 flat fillets of anchovy
¼ cup olive oil
36 very small white onions
2 tablespoons butter or margarine
2 cloves garlic, minced fine
4 sprigs fresh chervil or ½ teaspoon crushed dried chervil
2½ cups stock or bouillon
2 cups dry white wine
Lemon juice
Salt, pepper
1 cup hot fried croutons
Instant flour

Wipe and dry the doves. Truss by tying wings and legs close to body. Carefully insert an anchovy fillet between skin and meat on each breast, lengthwise. Heat the olive oil in a large cast-iron pot and lightly brown the birds on all sides. Do not overheat; cook slowly. In another pan, brown the onions in the butter, turning until nicely glazed. Add them to the doves. Add the garlic and chervil and slowly add the stock mixed with the wine. Cover tightly and simmer gently until birds are tender (about 40 minutes). Remove birds to heated platter and surround with onions and the hot croutons.

Keep warm while skimming excess fat from gravy. Thicken gravy slightly with a sprinkling of instant flour. Add a dash of lemon juice to the gravy and correct seasoning with salt and pepper to taste. Serve in bowl on side. Serves 4.
Serve with: crisp mixed green salad and wild rice, Fried Hominy (page 172) or Savory Wild Rice with Raisins (page 170).

Doves in White Wine Sauce

4 plump doves, split and flattened

3 tablespoons olive oil

3 tablespoons butter or margarine

1 cup dry white wine

½ teaspoon salt

¼ teaspoon freshly ground black pepper

4 chicken livers, chopped

4 small shallots or large scallions, chopped

2 whole cloves

1 cup sliced mushrooms, sautéed in butter

1 tablespoon minced parsley

Heat olive oil and butter in a large skillet and brown doves on both sides until golden. Pour in the wine and add salt, pepper. Cover and simmer for 20–30 minutes. Add all remaining ingredients except parsley and cook over medium heat, uncovered, for 10 or more minutes until birds are tender. Transfer birds to heated platter, pour sauce over, and sprinkle with parsley. Serves 4.

Serve with: new peas and tiny boiled potatoes.

Sherried Doves

8 small doves

Salt, pepper

4 tablespoons butter or margarine

1 clove garlic, minced fine

24 medium mushrooms, sliced

½ cup sherry (or port)

1 tablespoon flour mixed with 2 tablespoons pan juices

Melt butter in large cast-iron skillet. Season birds with salt, pepper and brown in the butter. Add garlic, mushrooms, and sherry and lower heat. Cover and simmer 15–20 minutes or until birds are tender. Transfer birds to heated platter and thicken the pan juices with the flour. Pour sauce over birds. Serves 4.

Serve with: fried toast triangles and watercress garnish.

Note: Recipe also good for pigeons.

Ptarmigan in Cream

3 ptarmigans or grouse, dressed
  Salt, pepper
6 strips bacon
½ stick butter or margarine
3 pints light cream
3 tablespoons red currant jelly or wild plum jelly

Wipe birds inside and out with paper towels. Sprinkle cavities lightly with salt and pepper. Tie 2 strips of bacon over each breast, using light butcher's cord. Melt butter in large heavy skillet and brown the birds on all sides. Transfer to large ovenproof casserole and pour in the cream. Cover and bake at 350° F. for about 1½ hours or until birds are tender. Lift out birds, split each in half, and lay on heated platter. Strain the pan gravy into a saucepan. Over high heat stir in the jelly until thoroughly melted (do not boil). Pour over birds and serve at once. Serves 3–6.
Serve with: crisp bacon slices and home-fried potatoes.

Ptarmigan in Mushroom Sauce

4 ptarmigans
  Flour
  Salt, pepper
½ teaspoon thyme
½ stick butter or margarine
1 cup small mushroom caps
1 can cream of mushroom soup
1 cup half-and-half
1 tablespoon chopped fresh parsley

Rinse and dry birds. Dust with flour and sprinkle with salt, pepper, and a little thyme. Melt butter in a heatproof covered casserole. Brown birds all over in the butter. Add mushrooms, cream of mushroom soup, and the cup of half-and-half. Cover and cook very slowly over low heat for about 45 minutes or until tender and done. Sprinkle with parsley; serve from casserole. Serves 4.
Serve with: Spicy White Cabbage (page 180).

Roast Prairie Chicken

 2 prairie chickens or grouse
 2 cups cooked hominy
 6 thick slices fatty bacon
    Salt, pepper
12 small white onions, peeled
12 small whole baby carrots, scraped
1½ glasses red wine
 1 cup Basic Brown Sauce (page 157)
24 button mushrooms sautéed in butter or margarine

Stuff birds with the hominy and close cavities. Wrap each bird in 3 slices of bacon and tie or skewer in place. Place birds in deep ovenproof casserole or roasting pan and sprinkle with salt, pepper. Arrange onions and carrots around birds. Roast in preheated 350° F. oven for 25–30 minutes for rare. Remove birds and vegetables and keep warm. Add wine to the pan juices and cook until liquids are reduced by half. Stir in brown sauce and mushrooms and heat through. Remove bacon strips from birds and return them to casserole with the vegetables. Serves 2–4.
Serve with: watercress or endive salad.

Of the millions of wild ducks taken annually by hunters, the mallard may well be the most popular and the most plentiful. Other favorites include the canvasback, redhead, black duck, pintail, teal, and the baldpate or widgeon. The mallard is the one most commonly found in game markets, and it is raised in pens for consumption. The rich dark meat of these birds is a true delicacy. Though there are heated arguments about how long (varying from 18 to 60 minutes) these birds should be cooked, most gastronomes concur that the meat should be rare with blood-red juices running; longer roasting toughens the fibers and dries out the flesh. There is also much controversy over whether or not to cover ducks with barding. One eminent chef says "never, but perhaps just a few thin slices of smoked ham" may be placed over the breast. Others recommend bacon covering, as does this book in many of the recipes. It is extremely important that these birds be kept moist during the cooking processes. Brushing with oil or butter or covering with bacon all help. This is doubly important for those who prefer long-cooking and a well-done duck.

Because of the diet of some ducks, the birds should be drawn promptly after being killed. The fishy aroma and flavor of a coot or scoter can be corrected by actually skinning the bird and/or soaking it or parboiling it and using it in a stew. Some schools of game cooking recommend that the bird be skinned and only the breasts be saved (the breasts are seared over hot coals or in a skillet with oil and then braised). This is a matter of taste, but simply filling the bird's cavity with deodorizing parsley, celery, apple, onion, and potato won't rid a highly fishy duck of the offensive flavor. Skinning and soaking are necessary and worth the effort, for a coot stew can be most delectable.

The flavor of duck meat is dictated by its diet and its diet by its habitat. The finest flavor is probably found in the shallow-water group of ducks which feed in grain fields and on the surface of the water. These include the mallard, black duck, teal, pintail, baldpate, and gadwall. Finest of the deep-water ducks is the canvasback which feeds on aquatic vegetation and crustaceans. Least palatable are the fish-eaters or the mergansers, which, while edible, are not particularly desirable.

Sizes of ducks vary considerably. A large plump mallard or canvasback can serve 2; on the other hand, the tiny teal might have to be served in pairs. For the most part, allow one duck per serving.

Simple Roast Duck

4 ducks, ready to cook
  Salt, pepper
2 small cooking apples, quartered
2 medium onions, peeled, quartered
4 celery stalk tops
½ stick butter, melted
½ cup Game Bird Stock (page 190)

Wipe and dry ducks. Sprinkle inside and out with salt, pepper. Insert in each cavity 2 quarters of apple and onion and 1 celery top. Place on rack in preheated 400° oven and roast for 20 minutes, basting three times with a mixture of the melted butter and stock. Ducks will be rare and crisp. Remove cavity contents and serve with sauce as desired, but do not prepare sauce from pan drippings. Serves 4–8.

Serve with: game accompaniments as suggested in Chapter IX (pages 169–190).

Note: Ducks will be more or less rare in the time specified, depending on their weight. This time is for the larger mallard species. If a more well-cooked bird is desired, continue roasting and basting until done, but do not overcook or the meat will toughen.

Braised Duck

2 large, old ducks, cut in serving-size pieces
  Flour
½ cup salad oil
1½ cups white wine
1 bay leaf
6 juniper berries, crushed
2 small onions, peeled, stuck with 2 cloves each
1½ teaspoons salt
3 tablespoons chopped fresh parsley
6 peppercorns, crushed

Coat duck pieces in flour. Heat oil in large, flameproof casserole and brown pieces on all sides. Add all remaining ingredients, cover and simmer until tender—about 1½–2 hours. Drain duck pieces and serve in casserole. Serves 4.
Serve with: Sauerkraut in Wine (page 178).

Honey-Orange Duck

2 large or 4 small ducks
  Salt, pepper
2 oranges, sliced thin (minus peel below)
1 stick butter or margarine
1 cup honey
1/4 cup brown sugar
1/2 cup lemon juice
2 teaspoons orange peel, shredded coarsely
1 tablespoon brandy (optional)
1 tablespoon prepared mustard
1/2 teaspoon powdered ginger
1/2 teaspoon pepper
1/2 teaspoon salt

Wipe ducks inside and out. Sprinkle cavities with salt, pepper. Divide sliced oranges and fill each cavity. Place, breast sides down, in roaster. Coat liberally with butter. Mix all remaining ingredients and pour over ducks. Cover and roast at 325° F. for 1 hour. Turn ducks breast sides up, baste with the honey mixture, cover, and roast for 30 minutes more. Remove cover, baste again, and roast 30 minutes more. Serve with the pan juices poured over. Serves 4.
Serve with: white or brown rice and spinach salad.

Pressed Duck

2 large mallards, with livers
  Salt, pepper
1 cup good dry red wine
1 tablespoon tart currant jelly (optional)
  Pinch cloves
2 teaspoons lemon juice
1/4 cup good brandy
2 tablespoons butter, cut in small pieces

Sprinkle birds with salt, pepper. Reserve livers. Roast birds in preheated 475° F. oven for 15–18 minutes. Carve breasts in thin slices and transfer to heated serving platter with juices. Then prepare the dish at the table: Pour 1/2 of the red wine into a chafing dish and add the breast slices with juices. Cover dish and turn up flame. Cut up the duck carcass and put all the pieces, the livers, pan drippings, remaining wine, jelly, cloves, and lemon juice into duck press. Press and add the brandy to the resulting juices. Heat sauce but do not boil. Pour over duck slices, dot with butter, and serve at once. Serves 2–4.
Serve with: Braised Endive (page 179).
Note: If desired, this dish may be flamed with 2 tablespoons heated cognac before adding butter and serving.

Duck with Rum Sauce

2 2-pound ducks
   Salt
1 pound cottage cheese
¼ teaspoon pepper
6 slices bacon
1 large onion, thinly sliced
1 tablespoon minced parsely
1 cup tangerine or orange juice
1½ cups dark rum
1 tablespoon flour mixed with 2 tablespoons water

Wipe and dry ducks inside and out. Sprinkle cavities with salt. Divide cottage cheese and spoon half into each duck cavity. Close with skewers. Lay ducks in shallow roasting pan, breast sides up. Sprinkle with pepper and cover with the bacon slices. Lay onion slices in pan and add the parsley, juice, and rum. Place in preheated 425° F. oven and roast for 30 minutes or to desired degree of doneness. Remove bacon slices and transfer ducks to heated serving platter. Remove cheese, stirring 2 tablespoons into pan juices over high heat. Stir in flour mixture and cook, stirring, till thickened. Serve on side as sauce, strained or as is. Serves 4.
Serve with: broiled orange slices and tender new peas.

Duck with Raisin Sauce

2 large mature ducks
2 stalks celery, tops included
1 large tart apple, quartered
   Salt, pepper
8 strips fatty bacon
1 cup apple juice or cider
1½ cups rosé wine
1 cup raisins
3 tablespoons red currant jelly or Wild Beach Plum Jelly
   (page 184)
1 tablespoon flour mixed to a paste in 2 tablespoons water

Wipe and dry ducks. Break up celery stalks and insert one in each bird's cavity. Add half the apple. Place birds, breast sides up, in a roasting pan. Sprinkle with salt, pepper, and cover birds with the bacon strips. Pour in the cider and wine. Add the raisins. Roast in preheated 375° F. oven for 40 minutes or until done to taste. Remove ducks to heated serving plate. Heat remaining contents of roasting pan to boiling and stir in the jelly and flour mixture. Lower heat to medium and continue to stir until mixture thickens to gravy consistency. Remove celery and apple from ducks. Split ducks lengthwise and pour sauce over them. Serves 4.
Serve with: Braised Endive (page 179) and wild rice.

Duck with Orange Sauce

2 large ducks (mallard or other)

2 cups Red Wine Marinade (page 153)

2 teaspoons salt

2 teaspoons powdered ginger or 2 teaspoons fresh, shredded
   ginger

½ teaspoon crushed or coarse-ground black peppercorns

1 teaspoon dried rosemary

2 whole oranges, quartered, seeded

1 tablespoon grated or shredded lemon peel

2 tablespoons brown sugar

½ cup curaçao

6 strips fatty bacon

1 tablespoon cornstarch, dissolved in 2 tablespoons cold water

¼ cup brandy, warmed

Marinate ducks for 3–4 hours, covered, in a cool place or in the refrigerator. Drain; reserve marinade. Dry ducks inside and out. Mix together salt, ginger, peppercorns, and rosemary. Rub surfaces of ducks with mixture. Divide oranges and insert in cavities. Add half of lemon peel and sugar to cavity of each duck. Place ducks in roasting pan and add 1 cup of the marinade and the curaçao. Cover breasts of ducks with the bacon strips and roast in preheated 350° F. oven for 45 minutes. Transfer ducks to heated platter. Remove and discard cavity contents and bacon. Heat pan drippings and stir in cornstarch mixture, thickening slightly. Pour brandy over ducks and ignite. Serve sauce on side. Serves 4.

Serve with: steamed white rice or Savory Wild Rice with Raisins (page 170) and Baked Stuffed Mushrooms (page 182).

Hungarian Roast Duck

2 large ducks (2–2½ pounds each)
1 clove garlic, split
  Salt, pepper
2 tablespoons paprika
2 apples, quartered, peels on
2 onions, quartered
6 slices bacon
1 stick butter or margarine, melted
3 cups sauerkraut
2 teaspoons caraway seeds
2 slices crisp cooked bacon, crumbled

Rub duck skin with garlic and sprinkle the birds inside and out with salt, pepper, and paprika. Fill cavities with the apples and onions. Cover breasts with bacon slices. Place birds, breast sides up, in roasting pan and bake at 350° F. for about 1 hour or until done to taste. Baste every 15 minutes with the butter. Meanwhile, mix together in a shallow baking dish the sauerkraut, caraway seeds, and bacon. Place in oven 15 minutes before ducks are done. To serve, discard apple and onion, and carve birds. Arrange slices on sauerkraut mixture. Serves 4.
Serve with: Spaetzle (page 173) or Parsley Potato Dumplings (page 174).

Rotisserie Ducks

3 large ducks (2½ pounds each)
3 small apples, cored, quartered
3 tablespoons butter or margarine
3 large sprigs parsley
3 small shallots, peeled
3 celery stalks
6 juniper berries
  Freshly ground black pepper
1 cup red wine
1 stick butter or margarine
½ cup brandy, heated
¾ cup Wild Beach Plum (page 184) or other tart plum jelly
1 tablespoon butter or margarine

Wipe birds dry inside and out. Stuff each with 1 apple, 1 tablespoon butter, 1 sprig parsley, 1 shallot, 1 celery stalk, and 2 juniper berries. Skewer or sew cavities closed. Place on spit close together. Rub with butter and sprinkle with pepper. Heat the red wine and the stick of butter and use as basting sauce. Roast on rotary spit for 20–30 minutes, basting frequently. Place birds on heated platter and pour brandy over. Ignite. Carve and serve with sauce made of jelly and butter heated together. Serves 6.
Serve with: Rice Pilaf (page 171) and mixed green salad.

Duck in Red Wine

2 ducks (2–2½ pounds each)
2 carrots, chopped fine
2 stalks celery, chopped fine
1 stick butter or margarine, melted
    Salt, pepper
2 medium onions, peeled
    Peanut oil
½ cup chicken broth
1 cup red wine
1 tablespoon cornstarch

Sauté carrots and celery in butter for 5 minutes. Make a bed of this in a roasting pan and sprinkle with salt, pepper. Tuck an onion into cavity of each duck. Brush ducks with peanut oil and place, breast sides up, on vegetables. Pour broth and wine around ducks. Roast at 400° F. for 25 minutes or until done to taste. Remove ducks to heated platter. Discard onions. Strain pan juices and heat, thickening with cornstarch mixed with water. Serve sauce on side. Serves 4. *Serve with:* wild or brown rice and Braised Celery (page 179).
Note: If ducks are small, allow 1 per serving and double the amounts of onions, carrots, celery.

Duck à l'Orange

2 ducks (2½ pounds each)
6 slices bacon
1 can (6 ounces) frozen orange juice, thawed, undiluted
1 clove garlic, minced
¾ teaspoon mustard
½ teaspoon ginger
½ teaspoon salt
1 tablespoon cornstarch
1 cup water

Wipe ducks dry inside and out and place in roasting pan close together, breast sides up. Cover with the strips of bacon. Roast at 400° F. for 25 minutes or until done to taste. Meanwhile, heat to boiling in small saucepan the orange juice, garlic, mustard, ginger, and salt. Remove from heat and, during last 10 minutes of roasting, remove bacon from birds and brush them with the mixture. Mix cornstarch with ¼ cup of the water and add to remaining orange sauce. Pour in remaining water and stir over low heat until sauce thickens. Place ducks on heated platter, slice, and serve with the orange sauce. Serves 4.
Serve with: Pecan-Rice Orange Cups (page 181) and watercress salad.

Duck Cantonese

2 ducks (2–2½ pounds each)
  Garlic salt, pepper
4 sprigs parsley
1 lemon, halved
6 slices bacon
½ cup beer
¼ cup dry mustard
2 tablespoons soy sauce
1 cup apricot or green gage plum preserves
¼ teaspoon ginger
1 tablespoon lemon juice
1 teaspoon grated orange peel
¼ cup melted butter or margarine

Wipe ducks dry inside and out and sprinkle with the garlic salt and pepper. Place 2 sprigs parsley and a lemon half in each cavity. Cover breasts with bacon slices and place in roasting pan. Make sauce by stirring together beer, mustard, and all remaining ingredients except butter. Heat in double boiler. Place ducks in 350° F. oven and roast for 30–35 minutes, basting frequently with the melted butter and once with the sauce. Transfer ducks to heated platter, carve, and serve with remaining sauce. Serves 4.
Serve with: steamed white rice.

Duck in Fruit Sauce

2 large mallards
  Salt, pepper
1 large tart apple, quartered
2 large stalks celery with tops, broken in 2-inch pieces
2 medium onions, quartered
8 slices fatty bacon
½ cup Game Bird Stock (page 190) or strong chicken broth
1 cup chopped blanched almonds
2 cups seedless green grapes
2 navel oranges or tangerines, peeled, pitted, segmented
1 teaspoon fresh lemon juice
1 tablespoon sweet butter
1 cup Madeira or port wine
¼ teaspoon freshly ground black pepper
  Pinch nutmeg
  Pinch allspice
½ teaspoon coriander seeds, crushed in a mortar
⅛ teaspoon powdered ginger
⅛ teaspoon cinnamon

Wipe ducks inside and out with a damp cloth dipped in a little of the wine. Sprinkle cavities with salt, pepper. Stuff each with half of the apple, celery, and onion. Place, breast sides up, in roasting pan and cover with the bacon slices.

Roast in preheated 350° F. oven for 10–15 minutes per pound for rare or 15–20 minutes for well done. Meanwhile, put in a blender all remaining ingredients except wine and whirl until smooth. Transfer mixture to saucepan and stir in the wine. Bring to a boil, stirring, but do not boil. Keep hot. Remove birds from oven when done and discard cavity contents. Split birds lengthwise, arrange on heated platter, and pour hot fruit sauce over. Serves 4.

Serve with: wild rice and Baked Stuffed Mushrooms (page 182).

Salmi of Duck

1 *large wild duck (2½ pounds)*
   Salt, pepper
4 *thick slices of bacon, diced*
1 *medium onion or shallot, sliced*
1 *bouquet garni (fresh thyme, marjoram, rosemary, parsley)*
1 *teaspoon butter or margarine*
1 *tablespoon flour*
1 *tablespoon butter or margarine*
1½ *cups stock or beef bouillon*
½ *cup claret*
6 *large green olives, chopped*

Wipe duck inside and out and sprinkle with salt and pepper. Fry bacon until crisp and put half of it and half of its fat in a roasting pan. Add onion, bouquet garni, and 1 teaspoon butter. Place duck on this, breast side down, and roast at 325° F. for 40 minutes. Meanwhile, melt the tablespoon of butter, stir in flour and heat, stirring, until brown. Slowly add stock, stirring, and then the claret, mixing until smooth. Bring to boil. Remove from heat. Cut off duck legs, wings, breast, and place in baking dish. Skim fat and stir pan gravy into the sauce. Add remaining bacon, olives, and the sauce to duck. Return to oven for 20 minutes. Serves 2.

Serve with: wild rice and Bavarian Cabbage (page 180).

Duck with Lentils

1 large mallard, black duck, or canvasback, with giblets
  Salt, pepper
3 tablespoons vegetable or olive oil
3 slices lean ham, diced (about 1 cup)
2 slices fatty bacon, coarsely chopped
1 small clove garlic, minced
1 medium onion, sliced thin
1 bay leaf, crumbled
1 tablespoon minced fresh parsley
1 large stalk celery, sliced in thin rounds
1 large carrot, sliced in thin rounds
¼ teaspoon pepper
½ teaspoon salt
⅔ cup white wine
3 cups cooked, drained lentils

Wipe and dry duck and sprinkle inside and out with salt, pepper. Chop giblets fine. Heat oil in Dutch oven and brown duck evenly on all sides. Add giblets and all remaining ingredients except wine and lentils and continue cooking and stirring over medum heat until vegetables become limp. Add wine and cook, stirring occasionally, until it has completely evaporated. Pour in boiling hot water to cover duck and continue to simmer slowly, covered, until duck is tender (about 1 hour.) Transfer duck to heated serving dish. Skim excess fat from pot and add lentils. Heat through. Surround and cover duck with the lentils and gravy. Serves 2–4.

Serve with: Stewed Apples (page 183).

Note: A large rabbit, disjointed, or 2 squirrels cut in serving-size pieces may be substituted for the duck.

Duck Soup

2 small ducks, cut in serving-size pieces

1 stick butter or margarine

Salt, pepper

1 cup diced, lean ham

1 cup chopped onion

2 medium carrots, diced

2 medium turnips, diced

1 beef bone, split and cracked

½ teaspoon thyme

1 bay leaf

6 peppercorns

1 teaspoon salt

2 tablespoons chopped fresh parsley

2 stalks celery, diced

Dash Worcestershire sauce

2 teaspoons tomato paste

½ cup cooked wild rice (optional)

Sherry

2 cups crisp-fried, cubed croutons

Brown the ducks in butter in a large soup kettle and sprinkle with salt, pepper. Add the ham and vegetables, stirring well and continuing to brown over medium heat. Place beef bone in pot and add enough water to cover. Add thyme, bay leaf, peppercorns, and salt. Cover and simmer for 2–2½ hours until duck is tender. Remove duck and set aside. Simmer 30–60 minutes more and remove beef bone. Return duck to pot and add parsley, celery, Worcestershire sauce, and tomato paste. Simmer until celery is tender. Add wild rice, heat through, and serve in soup bowls with sherry and croutons on the side. Serves 6.

Serve with: garlic French bread, if desired.

Note: 3–4 partridges or 2 small rabbits may be substituted for the ducks.

Black Duck in Wine

4 black ducks
3 tablespoons vegetable oil
1 tablespoon butter or margarine
1 large onion, sliced thin
1/4 teaspoon thyme
2 whole cloves
1 bay leaf, crumbled
3 peppercorns, crushed
1/4 teaspoon celery seed
1 teaspoon dried parsley flakes
1 cup sherry or vermouth
2 cups canned plum tomatoes
1/2 teaspoon salt

Heat oil and butter in a Dutch oven or heavy kettle with cover. Stir in the onion and all spices and herbs. Over medium heat brown the birds on all sides. Pour in the wine, lower heat, cover, and simmer for 20 minutes. Add the tomatoes and salt. Cover and continue to simmer for 1½ hours. Serves 4.
Serve with: brown or white rice.

Roast Coot

4 small coot, skinned
1 large tart apple, quartered
1 large potato, quartered
Tops of 4 stalks of celery
Salt, pepper
1/2 pound thin fat salt pork strips to cover birds
1 1/4 cups Simple Sauce Poivrade (page 158)

Wipe birds dry. Place in each cavity ¼ apple, ¼ potato, and 1 celery stalk top. Sprinkle birds with salt and pepper and wrap completely in fat strips. Roast in preheated 400° F. oven for 15–20 minutes. Remove fat strips and cavity contents from each bird and serve with hot sauce poivrade. Serves 4.
Serve with: Rice Pilaf (page 171).
Note: If birds have a very fishy smell, soak in salt water overnight.

Stewed Coot

2 coot, skinned, soaked in salt water overnight
3 thick slices fatty bacon, diced
4 large carrots, scraped, cut in 1-inch rounds
2 medium onions, diced
2 large, firm potatoes, cut in thick slices
1 tablespoon chopped parsley
1 tablespoon flour mixed with 2 tablespoons stew broth
  Salt, pepper

Drain and dry the birds. Cut into serving-size pieces. Cook bacon until light brown in a stew pot. Place bird pieces on top of bacon and just cover with water. Bring to boil, lower heat, cover, and simmer for 1 hour. Add carrots, onions, and potatoes and continue to simmer until vegetables are tender —about 20 minutes. Add chopped parsley and stir in the flour mixture. Simmer until liquids thicken, stirring to prevent sticking. Season with salt, pepper to taste. Serves 4.
Serve with: hot biscuits or corn muffins.

Roast Teal

4 teal, drawn and dressed
  Salt, pepper
2 medium, tart apples, cut in quarters
8 strips fatty bacon
1 cup red currant jelly
½ cup hot water
1 tablespoon cornstarch dissolved in 2 tablespoons water

Wipe birds dry and sprinkle inside and out with salt, pepper. Place 2 apple quarters in each cavity and wrap each bird in 2 strips of bacon. Put in roasting pan, breast sides up. Stir the jelly and hot water together and ladle over birds. Roast in preheated 350° F. oven for about 20 minutes, basting twice with the jelly. Birds are best served rare, but if desired, they may be cooked 5 minutes longer. (Warning: overcooking toughens.) Transfer to heated serving platter. Skim excess fat from roasting pan and thicken drippings with the cornstarch mixture, stirring over medium heat. Pour over birds and serve at once. Serves 4.
Serve with: wild or brown rice.

Casserole of Pintails

4 pintail ducks, dressed and drawn
1 stick butter, melted
4 large pats butter
1 medium onion, minced
1 shallot, minced
½ teaspoon crushed dried rosemary
    Salt, pepper
1 cup heavy cream
1 cup sour cream

Wipe birds dry. Brush with melted butter. Insert a pat of butter in each cavity. Put birds in roasting pan, sprinkle onion, shallot, rosemary, salt, and pepper over and around them. Roast in preheated 400° F. oven for 20 minutes, basting every 10 minutes with melted butter until birds are well browned. Transfer birds to ovenproof casserole. Put roasting pan over medium heat and pour in both cups of cream, stirring and scraping sides of pan to blend all the essences. When sauce is golden, pour over birds. Return to a 300° F. oven and bake until very tender and done (about 1 hour). Serves 4.

Serve with: Wild Rice Casserole (page 170).

Note: Recipe is especially suited to tough, older birds, and longer cooking will improve texture.

Among the numerous species of geese that winter in the United States are Canada, snow, white-fronted, and the small, dark brant. The young birds are especially prized as fine food and those that are truly wild, unlike their domestic cousins, are very lean, with dark, flavorful meat. Those that are pen-raised for sale in specialty markets have not had the exercise that the wild goose usually gets; hence they are less lean. Once in a while, a hunter will bring home an old goose that has grown lazy and done little flying. That one will be very tough and stringy and objectionably fatty.

Because geese are at their best during the holidays in England, they are traditionally served up at Christmas, simply roasted and stuffed with sage and onions. An average wild gander weighs between 8 and 14 pounds; the female, a pound or two less. It may be roasted with or without stuffing if it is a young goose, exactly as the domestic variety is treated. And if tender, it may be prepared in almost any way given for mallard or canvasback ducks, but it should be cooked longer. Whatever fat accumulates in the cooking of a wild goose should be drained; it is extremely strong.

Snipe are small birds with long beaks. Traditionally, when dressed, the heads are skinned and left on the bird, and the beaks are turned back and skewered through the bird so that it is self-trussed for roasting. These little birds have fine breast meat which should be covered with thin strips of fat salt pork to keep it moist. The snipe lives in marshy areas and is a clean bird, so that many epicures roast it without drawing it. It is rather like the woodcock in its habits (and looks like a smaller version), but the woodcock lives on wooded land near freshwater pools. The entrails of both these birds are sometimes eaten, and woodcock and snipe may be prepared similarly. A woodcock, however, is adequate for one person; two snipe make a single serving.

Virginia, clapper, and sora rail are all delicious little birds, but the Virginia is probably the most highly esteemed. The larger gallinule is also a member of the rail family. All of these may be handled and prepared like quail and snipe. The smaller species should be served 2 to a person; one of the larger rails is adequate for a single serving.

All-American Wild Goose

1 young wild goose (about 12 pounds), dressed
2 teaspoons salt
½ teaspoon freshly ground black pepper
6 cups cooked chestnuts, shelled and skinned
1½ cups melted butter
2 teaspoons salt
½ teaspoon pepper
1 teaspoon dried crushed sage
¾ cup cream
3 cups bread crumbs
4 tablespoons chopped parsley
1½ cups finely chopped celery
2 tablespoons grated onion
2 pints raw oysters, drained, cut in halves
8 strips bacon
½ cup gin
6 juniper berries
Instant flour

Rinse goose in cold water and pat dry inside and out with paper towels. Rub salt in cavity and on all surfaces of skin. Sprinkle with pepper. Set aside and prepare dressing: Put chestnuts through food mill or in blender. Combine them with the butter, salt, pepper, sage, cream, bread crumbs, parsley, celery, onion, and the oysters cut in halves. Fill goose cavity and close it with skewers or sew up the opening. Place goose in roasting pan, breast side up, and cover with bacon strips. Add gin and juniper berries to the pan. Roast at 375° F. for 15 minutes per pound or until goose is done to taste. Remove goose and keep warm. Skim fat from pan drippings. Heat drippings and sprinkle with a little instant flour, stirring until smooth and slightly thickened. Serve thickened drippings on side in bowl with the goose. Serves 6. *Serve with:* hot applesauce or Spicy White Cabbage (page 180).

Roast Goose with Sauerkraut

1 young goose (8–10 pounds), dressed, wiped dry
6 tablespoons lard or vegetable oil
1½ cups chopped onions
4 pounds sauerkraut, thoroughly drained
2 cups chopped tart apples
1 cup shredded raw potato (water pressed out)
2 teaspoons caraway seeds
¼ teaspoon pepper
½ teaspoon salt
8 strips fatty bacon

Melt lard in skillet and sauté onions until transparent. Add sauerkraut and simmer for 15 minutes, stirring once or twice. Cool and transfer to large mixing bowl. Add apples, potato, and seasonings. Mix lightly but thoroughly and fill goose cavity with the mixture. Close cavity. Truss legs close to body with butcher's cord. Cover breast with the bacon and place, breast side up, on rack in roasting pan. Roast at 325° F. for 25 minutes per pound or until goose when fork-tested yields yellow, not pink, liquid. Remove cord. Transfer to heated platter. Serves 6.
Serve with: Parsley Potato Dumplings (page 174).

Roast Goose, English Style

1 young goose (about 10 pounds), dressed, giblets reserved
   Salt, pepper
8 medium-to-small onions, peeled
1 bunch fresh sage, or 1 tablespoon dried crushed sage
8 slices thick bacon
   Flour
1 cup strong stock made from the giblets

Rinse goose thoroughly, drain, and pat dry. Sprinkle with salt, pepper inside and out. Fill cavity with the onions and the dried sage or several branches of the fresh sage. Sew or skewer cavity closed and tie ends of legs together. Place in roasting pan, breast side up, and cover with the bacon slices. Roast in preheated oven (325° F.) for about 2 hours. Sprinkle with flour and continue roasting until crisp and done (about 30 minutes more). Transfer to heated platter and keep warm. Skim fat from pan juices and add a tablespoon of flour to the juices, heating and stirring till smooth. Add the stock slowly, stirring. Bring to boil, and correct seasoning with salt, pepper to taste. Serve on side in bowl. Serves 6.
Serve with: hot applesauce or Fennel in Cream (page 177).

Roast Goose, German Style

1 young goose (about 10 pounds), cleaned and drawn; head,
    wings, neck, and feet removed
  Cold water to cover goose
  Salt, pepper
1 teaspoon crushed dried sage
4 cups water
1 onion, sliced
6 peppercorns
1/4 pound butter, melted, browned
2 tablespoons flour
2 cups water

Rinse and drain goose. Cover with cold water and let stand for 15 minutes. Drain and pat dry inside and out. Rub with salt, pepper. Sprinkle salt, pepper, and sage in the cavity. Place, breast side up, in roasting pan and add the 4 cups water, onion, peppercorns. Place in preheated slow oven (325° F.) and roast until water has evaporated. Then baste frequently with the butter. Roast for 2 hours and check degree of doneness. Continue till done. Transfer goose to heated platter and keep warm. Stir flour into pan liquids. Add 2 cups water, stir, and boil until smooth and thickened. Serve on side to pour over goose slices. Serves 6.
Serve with: Stewed Apples (page 183).

Roast Goose, Russian Style

1 small goose (8 pounds)
2 tablespoons salt mixed with 1 tablespoon thyme
6 medium apples, peeled, cored, and diced
1 teaspoon salt
1/2 teaspoon pepper
2 tablespoons minced fresh parsley
1 tablespoon sugar
1 1/2 cups strong chicken stock, bouillon, or consommé
2 medium onions, peeled, chopped fine
1 tablespoon flour mixed with 3 tablespoons water

Wipe goose dry inside and out. Rub cavity and all surfaces with thyme and salt mixture. Mix together apples, salt, pepper, parsley, and sugar. Stuff goose and close cavity. Place goose in roasting pan and pour in the stock; add onions. Roast in preheated 450° F. oven for 20 minutes. Reduce heat to 350° and roast for 1 1/2 hours or until goose is tender (fork-tested, its juices should run clear and legs should move very easily). Baste with pan juices every 15–20 minutes while roasting. When done, skim all excess fat from pan juices and thicken with the flour paste over medium heat. Serve on side in sauceboat. Serves 4.
Serve with: steamed kasha or buckwheat groats and baked apples.

Roast Goose, Hungarian Style

1 young goose (about 10 pounds)
  Salt, pepper
1 large head (3–4 pounds) red cabbage
3 tablespoons lard
1 large onion, sliced
1 tablespoon wine vinegar
1 cup red wine
1 tablespoon granulated sugar
1 large apple, cored, quartered
8 slices bacon

Wash and drain goose. Pat dry and sprinkle with salt, pepper. Set aside and prepare stuffing: Shred the cabbage. In a large iron skillet, melt the lard and sauté onions for a few minutes. Add the cabbage, vinegar, wine, sugar, and apple. Cook, stirring, over medium heat for about 10 minutes. Lower heat, cover, and simmer until cabbage is tender (about 1 hour). Drain and stuff cabbage into goose. Close cavity. Place goose in roasting pan, breast side up. Cover with bacon. Roast in preheated 350° F. oven for 20 minutes per pound. Transfer to heated platter. Skim fat from pan and thicken drippings with flour. Strain, reheat, and serve on side. Serves 6.
Serve with: Parsley Potato Dumplings (page 174).

Roast Goose, French Style

1 young goose (about 10 pounds)
  Salt, pepper
3 cups chestnuts cooked till very tender, peeled, sliced fine, or crumbled coarsely
2 large apples, cored, peeled, sliced very fine
8 slices bacon
  Flour

Rinse and dry goose thoroughly. Sprinkle cavity and skin with salt, pepper. Toss the chestnuts and apples together and fill cavity with the mixture. Close cavity with skewers or sew up. Place goose in roasting pan, breast side up, and cover with the bacon slices. Roast in preheated 350° F. oven for 20 minutes per pound or until done to taste. Remove bacon during last 20 minutes to brown breast. Transfer goose to heated platter and keep warm. Skim fat from pan juices. Sprinkle juices with flour, stirring till smooth and thickened. If necessary, strain to remove lumps; reheat. Serve on side. Serves 6.
Serve with: Stewed Apples (page 183) or Braised Escarole Amandine (page 182).

Broiled Breast of Goose

1 8-pound goose
1 cup dry white wine
½ teaspoon salt
¼ teaspoon freshly ground black pepper
½ teaspoon crumbled dry sage
1 bay leaf, crumbled
¼ teaspoon dried chervil or marjoram
1 teaspoon grated onion
2 tablespoons grated carrot

With a sharp boning knife, carefully remove both breasts of bird. Skin the breasts and place in bowl with mixture of all remaining ingredients. Let marinate, turning now and then so that all surfaces are permeated, for 8 hours or more (up to 2 days). Breasts will be like 2 steaks, approximately 4 x 2½ x 9 inches. Drain, pat dry, and broil in oven or over hot coals for 11 minutes on each side. Slice on an angle as for London broil. Serves 4.
Serve with: currant jelly, Wild Beach Plum Jelly (page 184), or broiled orange slices.
Note: Use carcass for making stock.

Hunter's Roast Goose

1 goose (10–12 pounds)
  Salt, coarse-ground black pepper
  Chestnut Stuffing (page 186)
½ pound fat salt pork, sliced thin
1 quart Game Bird Stock (page 190) or 1 quart beef bouillon
1 bay leaf
4 juniper berries, crushed
2 onions, coarsely chopped
2 stalks celery with tops, chopped
½ cup gin or genever
1 tablespoon cornstarch mixed with 2 tablespoons water

Wipe and dry goose inside and out. Rub surface and cavity with salt, pepper. Stuff and truss. Cover breast with the fat salt pork. Pour the stock into roasting pan and add all remaining ingredients except the cornstarch. Place goose, breast side up, on rack in the pan and cover. Cook in preheated 350° F. oven for 1½ hours, basting with pan juices every 20 minutes. Uncover and roast for 1 hour more, basting every 15 minutes. Transfer to heated platter. Skim fat from pan, remove bay leaf, and stir in cornstarch mixture, thickening over medium heat. Remove fat strips and trussing. Serve with gravy on side. Serves 6.
Serve with: Spiced Crab Apples (page 175).

Oven-Braised Goose

1 large old goose, giblets reserved
  Salt, coarse-ground black pepper
¼ cup bacon drippings
1 teaspoon crumbled dried sage
2 cloves garlic, mashed
2 cups dry red wine
6 cups Game Bird Stock (page 190) or beef bouillon
2 tablespoons flour blended with ¼ cup pan juices

Wipe goose inside and out and sprinkle liberally with salt, pepper on surface and in cavity. Chop the heart, liver, gizzard, and neck. Place goose under broiler and brown on both sides—about 10 minutes per side. Meanwhile heat bacon drippings in roasting pan and brown the giblets. Add sage and garlic and pour in wine. Bring to boil and put goose in pan, breast side down. Add stock and again bring to boil. Cover and cook in preheated 350° F oven for 2 hours. Turn goose breast side up, cover, and continue braising in oven for another 30 minutes or until goose is tender and done. Skim any excess fat and stir in flour mixture to thicken pan juices. Serves 8–10, depending on size of goose.

Serve with: Whipped Potatoes and Turnips (page 174) or Rice Pilaf (page 171) and Baked Apples (page 175).

Fruit-Stuffed Roast Goose

1 goose (10–12 pounds)
  Salt, fresh ground black pepper
1 tablespoon lemon juice
  Prune-Apple Dressing (page 188)
½ pound fat salt pork strips, sliced thin
1 tablespoon flour mixed with 2 tablespoons water
1 cup Game Bird Stock (page 190) or 1 cup bouillon

Wipe and dry goose inside and out. Rub salt and pepper into surface. Sprinkle cavity with lemon juice (or dip cloth in lemon juice and wipe). Fill with dressing, close cavity, and truss. Place on roasting rack in pan, breast side up, and cover with fat salt pork strips. Roast in preheated 350° F. oven for about 2¼ hours. Remove strips and continue to roast until breast is crisp—15–20 minutes more. Transfer to heated platter and keep warm. Remove excess fat from pan drippings. Blend in flour mixture and thicken drippings over medium heat, stirring constantly. Add stock, cook until thickened as desired for gravy. Serve on side. Serves 8.

Serve with: Butter-Crumb Noodles (page 172) and Braised Celery (page 179).

1 large goose (10–14 pounds)
  Juice of 1 lemon
4 cups dried white beans
1 pound salt pork, cut in large dice
1 large carrot, cut in 1-inch pieces
1 medium onion stuck with 3 cloves
3 cloves garlic
3 sprigs parsley
1/4 teaspoon thyme
1 bay leaf
1/2 teaspoon salt
1/4 teaspoon freshly ground black pepper
1 tablespoon tomato paste
6 small link sausages
1 small garlic sausage cut in thin slices
6 slices bacon
1/4 cup fine, dry bread crumbs

Carefully remove all breast meat from goose and cut in 1-inch-wide strips. Soak strips overnight in water to cover with lemon juice added. Place carcass in deep kettle, cover with water, and bring to boil. Simmer, covered, for 2 hours. Strain off and reserve broth. Soak beans in 2 quarts of water for 2 hours. Drain. Put in large kettle with cover and pour broth over. Broth should cover beans; if not, add sufficient water. Add all remaining ingredients except bacon and bread crumbs, cover and simmer for 1 hour. Beans should be almost done. If not, simmer longer. Transfer contents of kettle to large, ovenproof casserole. Lay bacon slices across top and sprinkle with the bread crumbs. Place in preheated 300° oven and cook for 1 hour more. Serves 6. *Serve with:* Stewed Apples (page 183).

Potato-Stuffed Roast Goose

1 goose (10–12 pounds)
1/4 cup vinegar
   Coarse sea salt
   Fresh-cracked white peppercorns
   Potato Stuffing (page 185)
1/2 pound fat salt pork strips, sliced thin
 2 cups Game Bird Stock (page 190) or bouillon
 1 teaspoon celery seed
 2 cloves garlic

Dip cloth in vinegar and wipe goose inside and out. Rub inside and out with the salt and peppercorns. Stuff and truss goose and place, breast side up, on rack in roasting pan. Cover with fat salt pork strips, pour in stock, and add the celery seed and garlic. Place in preheated 350° oven for 2 hours. Remove strips and continue to roast, basting every 10 minutes with pan drippings, until thoroughly done— about 30 minutes more. Serves 8.
Serve with: Gooseberry Sauce (page 164).

Potted Goose

2 cups cooked goose meat, fat, skin, bones removed
1 stick butter
   Pinch nutmeg
1/4 teaspoon fresh ground black pepper
1/2 teaspoon salt
 1 tablespoon cognac
 2 tablespoons melted butter

Put meat and butter through food grinder, grinding it twice and fine. Mix in remaining ingredients (except melted butter) and pack firmly into a heatproof crock or earthenware mold. Place in preheated 250° F. oven until heated through —about 25 minutes. Press down again with back of wooden spoon. Pour a thin layer of melted butter over surface and chill in refrigerator. Makes about 2¾ cups.
Serve with: crisp, dry toast or unsalted crackers.
Note: This is a good recipe for any leftover game birds.

Goose Liver Pâté

4 large goose livers or 12 duck livers
1 stick butter
2 tablespoons minced onions
½ teaspoon salt
   Pinch nutmeg
¼ teaspoon fresh ground black pepper
2 tablespoons cognac or good brandy
1 or 2 teaspoons coarsely chopped truffles (optional)

Melt butter in skillet and sauté livers until done through, but still quite pink inside. Drain and reserve 2 tablespoons of the butter. Lift out livers and set aside. Add onions to skillet and cook till transparent. Cool for a few minutes and pour skillet contents into blender. Add livers and all remaining ingredients except truffles. Whirl till smooth. Transfer to 1 pint crock and stir in the truffles. Pour reserved butter on top and chill. Butter will preserve the pâté for several weeks in the refrigerator. Makes about 1 pint.
Serve with: game bird dishes. Spread on toast, large croutons, or crisp-fried bread triangles.

Terrine of Goose

1 goose (8–10 pounds), liver included
½ pound lean ham, diced in ½-inch cubes
½ pound bacon fat, diced in ½-inch cubes
1 teaspoon salt
½ teaspoon freshly ground black pepper
   Juice of 1 clove of garlic
½ teaspoon dried thyme
1 teaspoon instant minced onion
¼ cup brandy
1 tablespoon butter
3 large shallots, peeled, chopped
½ pound lean fresh pork, ground twice
¼ pound lean veal, ground twice
½ pound pork fat, ground twice
½ teaspoon freshly ground black pepper
1 teaspoon salt
¼ cup brandy
3 eggs, lightly beaten
½ pound fat salt pork cut in thin slices

Completely bone the goose, leaving skin intact and removing breast halves in one piece. Cut breast meat in large dice (½- to ¾-inch cubes). Remove all of the rest of the meat from skin and bones and put through fine grind of food grinder twice. Place breast meat in large ceramic bowl and add the diced ham and bacon fat, 1 tablespoon salt, ½ teaspoon pepper, garlic juice, thyme, and minced onion. Pour brandy over and turn ingredients so that all surfaces are permeated. Refrigerate for 2–3 hours. Meanwhile, chop the goose liver and sauté it with the shallots in the butter. When liver is still pink but red juices have stopped running (2–3 minutes), remove from heat and allow to cool. Mix together the ground goose meat, pork, veal, fat, remaining pepper and salt, brandy, and eggs. Finally add the liver-shallot mixture and mix thoroughly. When diced meats have been marinated, combine the ground meat mixture with it. Line a terrine with the reserved goose skin (outer side down) and press in the meat mixture, pushing it down to fill all parts. Cover with the slices of fat salt pork. Place terrine in a pan with about 1 inch of water and bake at 300° F. for 2 hours. Fat on surface should be clear. Cool under a weighted plate overnight in refrigerator. Remove surface fat before serving in ½-inch slices. Serves 20–24.

Serve with: Melba toast and sweet butter, watercress and gherkin garnish.

Salmi of Goose

1 tough old goose, giblets included
1 tablespoon salt
2 large onions, sliced thin
3 large carrots, sliced thin
2 celery stalk tops, chopped
8 peppercorns
3 whole cloves
2 sprigs parsley
1 large bay leaf
½ teaspoon thyme
1 clove garlic, minced
  Port Wine Sauce (page 164)

Put all ingredients in a large kettle and cover with water. Bring to rolling boil, spooning off any scum on surface. Lower heat, cover, and simmer until goose is thoroughly cooked and tender—about 2½ hours. Cool, remove goose, and carefully cut all meat from the carcass in pieces as large as possible. Slice the breast in serving-size pieces. Heat the port wine sauce and add the meat, turning and coating each piece until all are warmed through. Serve at once. Serves 6–8.

Serve with: crisp toast spread with Goose Liver Pâté (page 128) and watercress garnish.

Roast Brant

2 large brant
1 lemon, quartered
  Salt, pepper
4 small onions, peeled and halved
1 teaspoon thyme
2 large carrots, cut in rounds
½ cup red wine
½ cup melted butter

Wipe and dry birds. Rub skin and inside with lemon and re-serve 2 lemon quarters. Sprinkle inside and out with salt and pepper. Let stand in refrigerator for 1 hour. Tuck a lemon quarter, 2 onions, ½ of the carrots, and a ½ teaspoon of thyme into each bird. Close cavities and place birds in shallow roasting pan. Pour in the wine and butter and roast in preheated 400° oven for 25–30 minutes or until done to taste. Split down the center to serve and discard cavity contents. Serves 4.
Serve with: Wild Rice Casserole (page 170) or Fried Hominy (page 172) and Currant Jelly Sauce (page 161).

Broiled Brant

2 large brant
  Juice of 1 lemon
  Salt, pepper
½ cup peanut oil
  Sauce Poivrade II (page 158)

Using poultry shears, cut birds down the back and open flat. Wipe, dry, and flatten with a cleaver. Brush with lemon juice and sprinkle with salt, pepper. Let stand for 30 minutes to 1 hour. Place skin side down on rack, brush with oil and cook under a preheated broiler at 550° F. for 8–10 minutes. Turn, brush again with oil, and broil for 8 minutes more. Birds should be rare. Cut in half, transfer to heated serving platter, and serve with sauce poivrade. Serves 4.
Serve with: Braised Celery (page 179) and Savory Wild Rice with Raisins (page 170).

Sautéed Snipe

8 snipe, heads, wings, feet removed
   Giblets from 8 snipe, chopped fine
1 stick butter
2 large shallots, minced
1 tablespoon minced fresh parsley
   Pinch nutmeg
   Salt, pepper
1 cup rosé or other light red wine
8 slices toast, trimmed, cut in triangles, buttered

Melt butter over medium heat in large skillet and when butter is foaming, add the chopped giblets, shallots, parsley, and nutmeg. Stir until giblets turn color, then add the snipe. Raise heat and brown snipe on all sides. Sprinkle with salt, pepper. Pour in wine, lower heat, cover, and simmer for 15 minutes or until snipe are tender but still rare. Transfer snipe to heated platter and pour pan sauce over them. Garnish and serve with the toast. Serves 4.
Serve with: buttered new peas and shoestring potatoes.

Snipe in Casserole

8 snipe, whole, ready to cook with heads skinned and beaks
   trussed through the legs
8 slices of bacon or thin slices of fat salt pork
   Salt, pepper
1½ sticks butter, melted
2 tablespoons brandy
8 pieces of toast fried in butter

Wrap each bird in bacon or fat slices and sprinkle inside with salt, pepper. Arrange, breast sides up, in a circle in a round casserole. Pour in and over all the melted butter. Place in a preheated 400° F. oven and roast, basting with the butter, for 10–12 minutes. (Birds are best when served rare.) Sprinkle each bird with a little of the brandy and serve on a piece of toast. Serves 4.
Serve with: julienned French fried potatoes and watercress.

Snipe Flambé

8 snipe, ready to cook whole or trimmed as desired
   Livers and hearts of snipe, chopped, cooked in butter
   Salt, pepper
8 slices bacon
8 thin slices of truffle (optional)
¼ cup melted butter
4 tablespoons brandy, warmed
1 teaspoon lemon juice

Wipe and dry the birds inside and out. Sprinkle lightly with salt, pepper. Wrap each in a slice of bacon. Tuck a truffle slice in each cavity (or insert between skin and flesh of breast, being careful not to break the delicate skin). Place breast up and close together in a shallow roasting pan and pour in the melted butter. Roast in a preheated 425° F. oven for 10–12 minutes, basting liberally with the butter. Birds will be rare. When done, transfer to heated serving platter. Remove bacon and cut each bird in half. Skim essences from roasting pan, pouring off excess fat, and place in saucepan with the cooked giblets. Add the lemon juice and 1 teaspoon of the brandy. Heat and serve on side. Bring birds to table, pour remaining brandy over them, and ignite. Serves 4.

Serve with: butter-fried toast and watercress.

Snipe-in-the-Bag

8 snipe, whole or trimmed as desired
   Salt, pepper
8 grape leaves
8 slices fatty bacon
2 cups fresh peas or 2 cups unthawed frozen peas
1 cup fresh, peeled, pearl onions or 1 cup unthawed frozen
   baby onions
1 cup thinly sliced fresh mushrooms
¼ cup port or sherry
¼ cup Game Bird Stock (page 190) or bouillon
2 tablespoons minced fresh parsley (optional)

Wipe and dry birds and sprinkle inside and out with salt, pepper. Place a grape leaf over the breast of each one and wrap a slice of bacon around it. Lay birds in an oven roasting bag in a shallow roasting pan. Add the vegetables to the bag and pour in the wine and stock. Close bag and pierce with cooking fork in 4–6 places to allow steam to escape. Roast in preheated 350° F. oven for 30 minutes. Transfer contents of bag with juices to heated casserole and serve at once. Serves 4.

Serve with: a simple green salad and hot biscuits.

Note: This method is suitable for all small game birds.

Broiled Rail or Gallinule

4 rail
½ cup flour mixed with 1 teaspoon salt, ½ teaspoon pepper
½ stick butter
1 tablespoon lemon juice

With poultry shears cut birds down the back. Flatten with a cleaver or chef's knife. Wipe and dry each bird; then dust with the flour mixture. Melt butter in large, heavy skillet and, when it foams, turn up heat and quickly brown birds on each side. Remove to broiler, reserving butter in skillet. Add lemon juice to skillet and use the lemon butter to baste birds as they are broiled for 4 minutes on each side (for rare). Serves 4.
Serve with: Fennel in Cream (page 177) and baked yams.

Roast Stuffed Rail

4 rail, ready to cook
1 pound chicken livers plus the rail livers, minced
1 medium onion, chopped fine, sautéed in butter
¼ pound bacon, minced, fried till golden, with drippings
4 large mushrooms, minced
1 tablespoon minced fresh parsley
1 cup coarse, dry bread crumbs
½ teaspoon salt (or more to taste)
¼ teaspoon freshly ground pepper
1 egg, lightly beaten
4 slices fatty bacon

Wipe and dry birds inside and out. Mix together all ingredients except the bacon slices and stuff birds loosely with the mixture. Place birds in shallow roasting pan, breast sides up, and cover with bacon slices. Roast in preheated 400° F. oven for 35 minutes or until done to taste. Baste with pan drippings twice. Serves 4.
Serve with: Orange Sauce (page 159) and green beans.

The series of charts on the next eight pages is designed for quick reference when you want to know: how long to freeze game and how to wrap it for storage; what handy equipment for the wild game cook is available in stores (where-to-buy list begins on page 211) and what substitutes can be used until you acquire the item you need; what the characteristics of a new-to-you game bird or animal are; what method of cooking should be used for which piece of game, how long to cook, approximate temperatures, how much to serve. How long to cook, of course, will vary according to the age of the wild game. Older flesh obviously will take longer. The size of a piece of meat or of a bird will also dictate time in the oven or on the stove. For the very best results, do not depend on the oven thermometer, but use a meat thermometer inserted in the fleshiest part of the meat. Read "venison" (and other antlered animal flesh) for beef, "pork" for bear, boar, collared peccary, hare, and rabbit.

The charts for cooking will serve best when you are creating your own wild game recipes. The freezing timetable will prove useful if you have bought or caught more game than you can use within a week or ten days.

Special Equipment for the Wild Game Cook

ITEM	SUBSTITUTE
Larding needle	Thin boning knife
Poultry shears	Cleaver, butcher knife
Hair or brass sieve	Cheesecloth, muslin
Marinade crock	Any large ceramic, glass, porcelain vessel or mixing bowl
Mortar and pestle	Spoon and bowl
Basting brush	Clean cloth on a stick
Meat thermometer	No substitute
Basting tube	Deep ladle
Pepper mill	No substitute
Skewers	Darning needle with heavy duty thread
Butcher's cord	Heavy string
Porcelainized roaster	Oven bags for roasts
Dutch oven, 8-quart size	Any large kettle with tight cover
Large cast-iron skillet with cover	Any big frying pan with cover
Terrines for pâtés, etc.	A glass loaf pan
Food and meat grinder	A friendly butcher
Chopping block table	Hardwood chopping board
Meat mallet	Rolling pin
Meat saw	Serrated knife
Duck press	Food ricer, heavy duty

Game Animal Characteristics

GAME	WEIGHT (pounds)	KIND OF MEAT
Antelope	100–140	Very lean, dark, like deer
Bear (black)	300–400	Beef-like, dark, sweetish flavor
Bison (buffalo)	up to 1 ton	Beef-like in texture, taste
Boar	300–350	Porklike, but much richer
Caribou	200–400	Like venison, but gamier
Elk	600–800	Dark, beef-like in taste, texture
Goat, Mountain	to 300	Kid goat like lamb
Hare	6–12	Rich, pleasantly gamey, dark
Moose	1300–1400	Beef-like but drier, darker
Muskrat	5–6	Dark, fine-grained, gamey
Opossum	to 10	Cross between pork/hare
Peccary, Collared	40–65	Light, dry, porklike
Rabbit, Cottontail (Marsh, Swamp, Brush, etc.)	2½–3½	Light, fine-textured, chickenlike
Rabbit, Snowshoe (or Varying Hare)	3–5	Very dry, dark
Rabbit (pen-raised)	2	Almost white, chickenlike
Rabbit, European	to 5	Light, darkens when cooked
Rabbit, Jack	6–10	Least palatable of rabbits, Whitetail best
Raccoon	12–25	Porklike, but less rich
Sheep, Dall	aver. 180	Rich, muttonlike

GAME	WEIGHT (pounds)	KIND OF MEAT
Squirrel, Fox	1½–3	Pink to pale red, lean
Squirrel, Gray	about 1	Pinkish, tender, sweet
Venison (deer)		
Whitetail	aver. 150	Beef-like but richer; tender if young
Florida Key	to 80	Tender, rich, cross between veal/beef
Mule	175–200	Gamier than others, dark, rich
Blacktail	up to 150	Beef-like, rich, dark
Woodchuck	aver. 10	Rich game flavor, dark

Game Bird Characteristics

GAME	WEIGHT	KIND OF MEAT
Brant	4–5 pounds	Dark, rich, gamey
Coot	2 pounds	Dark, rich, fishy
Dove	¾ pound	Flavorful, tender, medium dark
Duck (Mallard, Black, Pintail, Redhead, etc.)	2–2½ pounds	Dark, tender, fine-grained, rich, flavorful
Duck, Canvasback	2¾–3 pounds	Rich, dark, flavorful, tender
Gallinule	8 ounces plus	Rich, medium dark, aromatic
Goose (Canada, Snow)	to 14 pounds	Lean, dark, rich, flavorful
Grouse (and Prairie Chicken)	1¼–1¾ pounds	Very rich, medium dark, aromatic
Partridge	8 ounces–1 pound	White, flavorful, chickenlike
Pheasant (cock)	2¾–5 pounds	White breast, dark legs, fine texture, dense
(hen)	2–3 pounds	
Pigeon	1¼ pounds	Medium dark, flavorful
(squab)	12 ounces	
Ptarmigan	1–1½ pounds	Similar to grouse
Quail	6 ounces	White, delicately flavored
Rail	to 8 ounces	Medium dark, very rich, dense
Snipe	to 8 ounces	Medium dark, fine-textured, flavorful
Teal	10–12 ounces	Dark, fine-grained, flavorful
Turkey	up to 14 pounds	Very lean, rich, medium dark
Woodcock	8–10 ounces	Rich, medium dark, dense, leg meat white

Timetable for Freezing Game

GAME	MAXIMUM STORAGE		
Antelope	12 months	Pheasant (full-grown)	6 months
Bear	12 months	Pigeon	6 months
Bison (buffalo)	12 months	Ptarmigan	6 months
Boar	6 months	Quail	6 months
Brant	4 months	Rabbit	10 months
Caribou	12 months	Raccoon	6 months
Coot	4 months	Rail	7 months
Dove	5 months	Reindeer	10 months
Duck	4 months	Snipe	7 months
Elk	12 months	Squab (baby pigeon)	7 months
Gallinule	6 months	Squirrel	10 months
Goat	8 months	Teal	4 months
Goose	4 months	Turkey	8 months
Grouse	6 months	Venison	10 months
Hare	10 months	Woodchuck	6 months
Liver (big game)	3 months	Woodcock	7 months
Liver (small game, birds)	4 months		
Moose	12 months		
Muskrat	6 months		
Opossum	6 months		
Partridge	8 months		
Peccary	6 months		
Pheasant (baby, 1–1½ pounds)	8 months		

Note: Store minced or ground meat no longer than 3 months. Freeze stock in ice cube trays and bag them (6 cubes equal 1 cup). Freeze birds promptly; age big game for 2 days in refrigerator before freezing. Freeze giblets wrapped separately inside cavities of birds. The older the bird, the quicker it should be used. Use aluminum foil or polyethylene bags; remove as much air as possible and be sure that packages are moistureproof and airtight. Keep freezer temperature no higher than 0° F.

Game Bird Cooking Guide

GAME	AMOUNT PER PERSON	METHOD	TEMPERATURE/TIME	
Brant	1 pound	Roast, rare	400° F.	30 min.
		Roast, well	350–375°	1½ hrs.
		Broil	550°	18 min.
		Braise, stew		2 hrs.
Coot	1 pound	Stew		1½ hrs.
Dove	1 bird	Roast	400° F.	20 min.
		Braise (oven)	300°	1 hr.
		Braise		up to ½ hr.
		Broil	550°	12 min.
Duck	1–1½ pounds	Roast, rare	400° F.	20 min.
		Roast, well	400°	50 min.
		Broil	550°	15 min.
		Stew		1½ hrs.
		Braise		up to 2 hrs.
Gallinule	1–2 birds	Broil, rare	550° F.	8 min.
		Roast, well	400°	30–35 min.
		Braise		40 min.

GAME	AMOUNT PER PERSON	METHOD	TEMPERATURE/TIME	
Goose	1–1½ pounds	Roast	375–400° F.	2–3 hrs.
		Braise		2 hrs.
		Stew		2½ hrs.
Grouse	½–1 bird	Roast	350–400° F.	15–30 min.
		Broil, split	550°	15 min.
		Braise, oven	300–325°	1–2 hrs.
Partridge	1–2 birds	Roast	400° F.	15–40 min.
		Braise, oven	325°	1½ hrs.
Pheasant	1 lb.	Roast	350–375° F.	30–40 min.
		Roast, stuffed	350°	1½ hrs.
Pigeon	½–1 bird	Roast	350–400° F.	20 min.
		Braise		45–50 min.
Pigeon (squab)	1 bird	Roast	400°	20 min.
		Braise, etc.	(See Dove)	
Ptarmigan	½–1 bird		(See Grouse)	
Quail	2 or more birds	Roast	375–400° F.	20–30 min.
		Braise		30–45 min.
		Broil	550°	15–30 min.

GAME	AMOUNT PER PERSON	METHOD	TEMPERATURE/TIME
Rail	2 or more birds	Roast	400° F. 20–35 min.
		Broil	500° 8 min.
		Braise	30–40 min.
Snipe	2 birds		(See Gallinule)
Teal	1 bird		(See Duck)
Turkey	1–1½ pounds	Roast, stuffed	350° F. 20 min. per pound
		Braise	2–3 hrs.
Woodcock	1 bird	Roast	350° F. 20–35 min.
		Braise	45 min.
		Broil	500–550° 8–10 min.

General Tips on Cooking Game Animals

Individual recipes for cooking game meat will indicate cooking times and temperatures for specific cuts. In general, the amounts to serve per person are as follows:

> 1 pound of boneless meat = 4 servings
> 1 pound of meat, few bones = 3 servings
> 1 pound of meat, much bone = 2 servings

Big game is butchered very much like domestic beef, veal, et al. *Boneless meat* includes such cuts as flank steak, all boneless roasts, fillets, ground meats, and liver. *Meat with few* or *small bones* includes: round steak and pot roast, slices from the ham of the animal. *Meat* with a *large quantity* of *bone* includes most steaks, shoulder cuts, rib and neck chops, breast, racks of small animals.

Tough meats should be cooked by stewing or braising; moisture and long, slow cooking render these cuts tender, and the addition of herbs, spices, vegetables and other seasonings heightens flavor. Young meat—from young antlered animals—may be cooked as any prime beef is cooked. Since most wild game is dry, additional fat must be added in the cooking. Roasts are distinctly enhanced by larding (page 200) or cooking with some of the marinade in which they have been tenderized for a while.

The word "marinate" comes from the Spanish and means, literally, "to pickle." Pickling means to preserve, soften, and flavor. And marinating does just that. An old tough bird or piece of meat may be tenderized and enhanced to great palatability by being steeped in a marinade. A too-gamey-tasting animal can be brought to better flavor with a good marinade. The acid marinades are the ones that do the tenderizing, those that contain a proportion of acid in the form of vinegar, wine, or lemon juice. Depending on the bird species or cut of game meat, marination may take any-where from an hour or two up to a week or more.

The technique of marinating is simple enough, but certain things are important: 1) While there should ideally be enough marinade to cover, halfway up is sufficient if the meat or bird is turned often enough. 2) Only glass, porcelain, or ceramic containers should be used for marinating purposes; metal reacts with the acids and can impart undesirable flavors. 3) After immersion, the meat or bird should be turned frequently so that all surfaces are permeated, and the marinade should be stirred at each turning. 4) While mari-nating, the meat or bird should be covered and kept in a cool place, though not necessarily refrigerated.

Often a marinade—especially one with a good proportion of wine among the ingredients—may be used for basting a roast or bird, as well as for making a sauce or gravy. Among the recipes for sauces and gravies on the next pages is a wide variety, with suggested uses for each. The best of all sauces enhance, never mask, the flavors of wild game. Nor should game be drowned in gravy or overpowered by its flavor. Whenever possible, a sauce or gravy should be made with the essences, juices, and pan drippings from the game itself. If a recipe calls for stock, then it should be stock made from the bones and meat of the animal being prepared or the bones, giblets, and flesh of the bird to be served. Substitutes, of course, may be necessary in some cases and these are indi-cated in the recipes. If wine is called for in the preparation of a sauce, then honor the bird or beast with a good wine— not a so-called "cooking" wine. It need not—and should not —be the rare vintage bottle planned for the table, but it should be compatible. And further do justice to the gastro-nomic treat to be served by using the best quality ingredients you can buy.

Simple Marinade I

1 cup dry white wine or wine vinegar
¼ cup salad oil
½ teaspoon pepper
1 teaspoon salt
1 tablespoon grated onion

Mix all ingredients together and pour over meat or bird to be marinated. Makes 1¼ cups.

Note: Marinade may be doubled or tripled for larger cuts of game.

Simple Marinade II

1 cup red or white wine
¼ cup white or cider vinegar
¼ cup water
½ teaspoon salt
¼ teaspoon pepper
1 onion, halved and stuck with 2 cloves

Mix all ingredients together and pour over meat or bird to be marinated. Makes 1½ cups.

Quick Game Marinade

1 8-ounce bottle French dressing
1 teaspoon dried parsley flakes
¼ teaspoon dried basil
¼ teaspoon dried savory
¼ teaspoon dried marjoram
½ teaspoon dried chopped chives

Mix all ingredients together and pour over meat or bird to be marinated. Makes 1 cup.

Dry Game Marinade

1 cup wine vinegar
1 cup peanut oil
1 bay leaf
¼ teaspoon thyme
¼ teaspoon celery seed
¼ teaspoon pepper
½ teaspoon salt
1 clove garlic, mashed (optional)

Mix all ingredients together and pour over meat or bird. Use for those game birds or meat which are extremely dry and lean. Makes 2 cups.

Note: Recipe may be halved to make 1 cup; or doubled to make a quart to tenderize a tough, dry game roast.

Tough-Meat Marinade

1 cup red wine
½ cup cider vinegar
1 medium onion, sliced thin
1 clove garlic, crushed
1 cup water
1 medium carrot, sliced in thin rounds
3 peppercorns
½ teaspoon salt
2 sprigs parsley
2 celery stalk tops
¼ teaspoon crushed rosemary
¼ teaspoon thyme
1 bay leaf

Mix all ingredients together and pour over meat in a glass or ceramic bowl. Store, covered, in a cool place or in the refrigerator for 2–4 days. Turn meat every 4–5 hours so that all surfaces are permeated by the marinade. Makes about 2¾ cups.

Fatty Game Marinade

¾ cup lime juice
½ cup orange juice
½ cup vinegar
2 cups apple cider
1 medium onion, sliced thin
1 cup diced celery
1 large carrot, diced
1 clove garlic, minced fine
2 tablespoons chopped fresh parsley
1 bay leaf
¼ teaspoon nutmeg
2 seeded chili peppers (optional)

Mix all ingredients together and pour over fatty game such as bear, wild boar, collared peccary to marinate for 3 hours or more. Makes about 4½ cups.
Note: Recipe may be halved as necessary.

Red Wine Marinade

1½ cups vegetable oil
½ cup finely chopped onions
1 shallot, minced
1 clove garlic, minced
1 large stalk celery (top included), diced
1 large carrot, sliced thin
1 tablespoon minced fresh parsley
1 bay leaf
8 peppercorns
8 crushed juniper berries
1 pinch thyme
1 pinch rosemary
3½ cups red wine

Heat ¼ cup of the oil in large skillet. Add and sauté vegetables, herbs, and spices until the onions are clear and golden. Remove from heat and stir in remaining oil and wine. Cool and pour over meat. Makes enough for about 5 pounds of venison, antelope, elk, bear, moose, et al.

White Wine Marinade

1 large onion, sliced thin
1 large carrot, sliced thin
1 clove garlic, minced
½ bottle dry white wine
1 tablespoon chopped fresh parsley
1 large bay leaf, crumbled
6 peppercorns, crushed
½ teaspoon thyme
½ teaspoon basil
3 tablespoons olive oil
1 tablespoon salt

Mix all ingredients together and pour over meat. Makes about 2½ cups.

Juniper Marinade

1 cup red wine
¼ cup gin
1 cup vegetable oil
6 crushed juniper berries

Mix ingredients together and pour over venison, game birds, or small, tough game animals. Makes 2¼ cups or enough for 6–8 pounds of meat or birds.

Sherry Marinade

1½ sticks butter or margarine, melted
2 tablespoons juniper berries, lightly crushed
2 teaspoons coarse cracked pepper
6 whole cloves
3 cups sherry

Mix all ingredients together and pour over pheasant, coot, duck, venison, moose, or bear meat. Makes about 4 cups.
Note: Use also as a basting sauce.

Venison Marinade

1 cup vinegar
½ teaspoon dried sage
½ teaspoon thyme
1 teaspoon dried mint or 1 tablespoon chopped fresh mint
2 tablespoons minced onion
2 cups olive or vegetable oil

Soak the herbs and onion in the vinegar overnight. Combine the mixture with the oil and pour over the venison, turning to coat all sides. Cover and allow to marinate overnight or longer, depending on toughness and age of meat. Makes 3 cups.

Note: For smaller cuts of meat or for other small game this marinade may be halved.

Big Game Marinade

3 large onions, coarsely chopped
4 large shallots, chopped
3 large carrots, cut in thin rings
3 stalks celery, chopped (tops included)
¾ cup tarragon wine vinegar
1 tablespoon salt
2 cloves garlic, minced
12 crushed peppercorns
2 large bay leaves, crumbled
1 bottle dry white wine

Put all ingredients in a large saucepan and bring to a boil. Lower heat and simmer for 5 minutes. Cool and pour over game pieces. Makes about 5 cups.

Use for: bear, venison, elk, moose, sheep, goat, buffalo.

Note: Recipe may be halved for smaller cuts of game.

Hot Marinade

2 cups dry red wine
1 tablespoon finely chopped parsley
½ teaspoon thyme
1 teaspoon pepper
1 medium onion, sliced thin
1 clove garlic, minced fine
½ teaspoon powdered cloves
2 large bay leaves, crumbled
6 whole allspice, crushed

Bring all ingredients to boil and cook over high heat for 5 minutes. Pour boiling hot over game to be marinated and let stand for 2–4 hours. Makes about 2 cups.

Use when: there is not enough time for long marinating of dry, tough game cuts.

Oriental Marinade

¾ cup soy sauce
¼ cup sherry
¼ teaspoon powdered ginger
1 teaspoon sugar
1 clove garlic, minced fine

Mix all ingredients together and pour over meat or bird to be marinated. Makes 1 cup.

Note: To double quantity, double all ingredients except the garlic.

Basic White Sauce

1 stick butter or margarine
3 tablespoons flour
2 cups hot milk
1/2 teaspoon salt
1/2 cup light cream, heated but not boiled (optional)

Melt butter over medium heat. Blend in flour till smooth and slowly add, stirring, the hot milk. Add salt and continue stirring until sauce is thickened as desired. Add and blend in the cream for a richer, creamier sauce and continue to cook, stirring, until thickened. Makes 1½–2 cups. *Use for:* all sauce recipes calling for basic white sauce.

Basic Brown Sauce

2 tablespoons butter or margarine
2 tablespoons flour
2¼ cups beef or game stock, bouillon, or consommé
    Salt, pepper

Melt butter and blend in flour, cooking and stirring over low heat until mixture is light brown. Gradually add the stock, stirring until smooth. Over medium heat, bring to boil, stirring rapidly for 3–4 minutes. Lower heat and simmer for 20 minutes, stirring now and then to prevent sticking. Remove from heat and season with salt, pepper to taste. Makes about 2 cups.
Note: Use this basic sauce when making mushroom, poivrade, currant jelly, wine, and other sauces.

Simple Sauce Poivrade

1 tablespoon butter or margarine
2 shallots, coarsely chopped
¼ teaspoon coarsely ground black pepper
1 tablespoon fresh lemon juice
1 cup pan drippings from game roast, fat skimmed off
    Stock or bouillon

Melt butter in saucepan and sauté shallots until golden. Season with pepper. Add lemon juice and pan drippings (plus enough stock to make 2 cups of liquid). Boil over high heat until liquid is reduced to about 1¼ cups. Makes 1¼ cups.

Sauce Poivrade II

1 stick butter or margarine
1 medium onion, chopped fine
1 medium carrot, chopped fine
1 clove garlic, crushed
2 teaspoons minced parsley
¼ teaspoon thyme
1 bay leaf, crumbled
½ cup white or red wine
1 cup Basic White Sauce (page 157)
1 cup Basic Brown Sauce (page 157)
1 tablespoon tomato paste
8 peppercorns crushed in a mortar
3 tablespoons currant jelly

Melt butter in large skillet and sauté onion and carrot until golden. Add garlic, parsley, thyme, bay leaf, and wine. Simmer until liquid is reduced by half. Add brown and white sauces, tomato paste, and peppercorns, stirring occasionally over very low heat for 1 hour. Remove from heat and force through strainer. Return strained sauce to pan over medium heat and bring to boil. Stir in the jelly, heat through, and serve with venison, elk, antelope, wild duck et al. Makes about 2 cups.

Bread Sauce

1 small onion, peeled and stuck with 3 whole cloves
1 whole bay leaf
1 pint milk or half-and-half
1½ cups finely crushed dry bread crumbs
½ teaspoon salt
⅛ teaspoon cayenne
2 tablespoons butter or margarine

Put onion, bay leaf, and milk in a saucepan and bring to a boil. Add the crumbs, salt, and cayenne and simmer for 2–3 minutes. Remove bay leaf and onion. Beat in the butter until mixture is smooth and creamy. Serve hot. Makes about 2½ cups.
Serve with: roasted small birds.

Orange Sauce

2 tablespoons fat from roasting pan or 2 tablespoons butter or margarine
3 tablespoons flour
1 cup hot Game Bird Stock (page 190) or bouillon
½ cup orange juice
1 tablespoon finely shredded orange peel
1 teaspoon lemon juice
1 tablespoon sherry or port
Pinch cayenne

Heat fat or butter in saucepan and blend in the flour, stirring until golden but not dark brown. Gradually add the stock, stirring over medium heat until thickened. Stir in all remaining ingredients and heat through. Makes about 1½ cups.
Serve with: pheasant, quail, snipe, rail, and other game birds.

Mint Vinaigrette Sauce

1 cup cider vinegar
½ cup sugar
¼ teaspoon salt
½ cup finely chopped fresh mint (packed tight)

Heat vinegar and dissolve sugar and salt in it. Stir in the mint and cool. Makes about 1¾ cups.
Serve with: hot or cold roast venison, elk, sheep, antelope.

Wine Sauce

2 cups Basic Brown Sauce (page 157)
⅓ cup wine: red, Madeira, sherry, vermouth, or other

Heat brown sauce over medium heat, stirring, until it is reduced to about 1½ cups. Add the wine and bring to the boiling point, but do not boil. Serve at once. Makes about 1¾ cups.

Currant Jelly Sauce

1 cup Basic Brown Sauce (page 157)
¼ cup currant jelly

Heat brown sauce and stir in the jelly, blending and cooking over low heat until smooth and hot. Makes 1¼ cups. *Use for:* venison, bear, elk, and other dark-meated large and small game.

Piquant Currant Jelly Sauce

1 cup tart red currant jelly
½ stick butter or margarine
1 tablespoon freshly grated horseradish

Put all ingredients in a saucepan and stir over low heat until melted and well-blended. Serve hot. Makes 1½ cups. *Serve with:* venison or other big game chops, cutlets, or roast; duck, brant, quail, grouse, partridge, and other small game birds prepared without other gravy or sauce.

Mushroom Sauce

1 cup cream sauce (Basic White Sauce, page 157) or Basic
    Brown Sauce (page 157)
½ stick butter or margarine
1 cup sliced fresh mushrooms
    Salt, pepper

Melt butter and sauté mushrooms until golden. Heat cream sauce and add mushrooms. Add salt, pepper to taste. Makes 2 cups.

Use with: cooked breasts of pheasant, turkey, and white-meat game birds.

Sour Cream Sauce I

1 shallot, chopped fine
2 tablespoons butter or margarine
1 tablespoon flour
1 cup stock or chicken bouillon
3 tablespoons white wine
2 tablespoons sour cream
    Few drops of lemon juice

Sauté shallot in butter in small saucepan. Add flour and blend till smooth. Slowly add stock or bouillon, stirring; then blend in the wine. Cook slowly over low heat until thickened (10–15 minutes), stirring continually. Add sour cream, taste, and add lemon juice as desired for flavor. Serve hot. Makes about 1¼ cups.

Use with: bear, venison, upland game birds.

Sour Cream Sauce II

2 tablespoons butter or margarine
¼ cup minced onion
½ cup beef stock, bouillon, or consommé
2 cups sour cream, warmed
1 tablespoon red currant jelly (optional)

Melt butter and sauté onion until soft. Add stock and stir over medium heat until liquid has almost evaporated. Add sour cream to the onion mixture, stirring over low heat for 3–4 minutes. Remove from heat and stir in the jelly, if desired. Makes about 2 cups.

Note: For game recipes with tomato or tomato sauce, omit the jelly.

Fruit Sauce

1 cup seedless grapes
1 cup dried apricots, chopped
1½ cups water
½ stick butter or margarine
½ cup Madeira wine
¼ teaspoon cinnamon
   Pinch of cloves
   Pinch of nutmeg
½ teaspoon powdered ginger
¼ teaspoon salt
½ cup ground or finely chopped nuts (almonds, hickory, pecans)

Cover grapes and apricots in saucepan with water and bring to boil. Lower heat and simmer for 10 minutes. Drain fruit and add all remaining ingredients. Simmer for 10 minutes. Makes about 2½ cups.

Use with: roasted small game birds, duck, turkey, and deer, bear, elk, moose chops and steaks.

Gooseberry Sauce

1 pint green gooseberries
¼ cup water
¼ cup sugar
½ teaspoon lemon juice

Clean and pick over the gooseberries. Wash, drain, and put in saucepan. Add water, sugar, lemon juice. Mash down with potato masher and cook over medium heat, stirring, for 10–15 minutes. Strain through coarse sieve. Makes 2 cups.
Use with: small game birds, turkey, goose, duck.

Port Wine Sauce

1 cup defatted, strained pan drippings from roast game birds
    or 1 cup Basic Brown Sauce (page 157)
1 cup port
1 small shallot, chopped fine
1 tablespoon minced fresh parsley
¼ teaspoon thyme
½ cup fresh orange juice
2 tablespoons lemon juice
1 teaspoon shredded orange peel
1 teaspoon shredded lemon peel

Combine drippings or brown sauce in saucepan and bring to boil. Lower heat, add shallots, and simmer for 5 minutes. Add all remaining ingredients, turn up heat and boil, stirring, for 5 minutes more. Makes 2 cups.
Serve with: all game birds.
Note: If drippings are not thick enough, stir in 1 tablespoon cornstarch mixed with 2 tablespoons water just before final 5 minutes of cooking.

Prune Gravy

2 cups skimmed pan drippings from roast goose, duck or turkey
2 tablespoons flour
3 tablespoons cold water
12 stewed prunes, pitted and coarsely chopped

Bring drippings to a boil and quickly stir in the flour mixed smoothly with the cold water. Add the prunes, stirring, and bring again to a boil, but do not boil. Serve with game birds on the side. Makes about 3 cups.

Note: If sufficient drippings are not available, add enough chicken broth or stock to make 2 cups.

Sweet-Sour Basting Sauce

1 cup vinegar
1 cup brown sugar
1 cup water
1 cup canned crushed pineapple
1 cup canned plum tomatoes, drained
1 large green pepper, seeded and diced
1 teaspoon dry mustard
2 tablespoons soy sauce
1 tablespoon cornstarch, dissolved in 2 tablespoons water

Place all ingredients except cornstarch in saucepan over medium heat. Stir and bring to boil. Lower heat and simmer sauce for 15 minutes. Stir in the dissolved cornstarch and continue stirring over medium heat until sauce becomes translucent and coats spoon. Makes about 1 quart.

Use for: basting grilled bear steaks, spitted small game birds, wild boar.

Basic Rotisserie Sauce

½ cup vegetable oil
½ cup lemon juice or wine vinegar
 1 large clove garlic, minced fine
 2 tablespoons minced onion
½ teaspoon salt
½ teaspoon freshly ground black pepper

Shake all ingredients together in a screw-top jar. Refrigerate overnight. Shake again before using. Brush on spit-roasted or grilled turkey and small game birds. Makes about 1 cup.

Tarragon Barbecue Sauce

½ cup vegetable oil
½ cup fresh lime juice
 2 tablespoons grated onion
 2 teaspoons chopped fresh tarragon
   Pinch pepper

Shake all ingredients together in a screw-top jar. Brush on and baste broiled turkey and small game birds during cooking on spit or grill. Makes about 1 cup.

Most wild game dishes need accompaniments that balance or point up flavors of the meat. The palate-piquing traditional foods include tart jellies, sweet-sour red cabbage, sauerkraut, spicy white cabbage, savory wild rice, chestnuts whole and chestnuts puréed, braised celery or endive or escarole, stewed apples or applesauce, grapes, oranges and lemons, cranberries, squash, yams and sweet potatoes, and a score of others. All of these in one guise or another are represented in the recipes that follow. In addition, there are some new ideas which may not have entered your kitchen such as Rosemary Onions, Brussels Sprouts with Grapes, and Fennel in Cream.

Then there are suggestions for various kinds of dressings and stuffings which are traditionally used with certain game birds. And finally, there are two basic recipes for making stock—one for big game and one for game bird stock.

Since many people eat with their eyes first, then savor, do not overlook garnishing touches when serving your wild game masterpieces. Watercress garnish and fried toast triangles are traditional for many birds, especially the smaller ones. The toast not only looks attractive, but it also serves the purpose of catching the delicious bird juices. Garnishes should not only delight the eye and the palate, but they should complement the flavor of the dish. Consider rimming a magnificent roast goose with spiced crab apples or a crisply browned mallard with kumquats. Garnish a quail with a little cluster of fresh green grapes or a holiday wild turkey with tiny molds of jellied whole cranberry sauce wreathed around it. Avoid going overboard, however, since the bird or beast must not be upstaged. Sometimes, just the simplicity of accompanying vegetables—tiny onions, baby carrots, little new potatoes—makes the picture perfect.

Wild Rice Casserole

½ cup raw wild rice
½ cup brown rice
   Boiling water
3 cups game stock or beef or chicken consommé
   Salt, pepper
1 cup shelled walnuts, coarsely broken by hand
1 large apple, pared, cored and chopped fine
1 tablespoon minced fresh parsley
1 tablespoon butter or margarine

Rinse wild rice in cold water. Drain. Mix together with the brown rice and pour boiling water over to cover. When cool, drain. Repeat twice and finally drain very thoroughly by pressing rice down in a sieve. Bring stock or consommé to boil, add rice and simmer, covered, without stirring until rice is tender and moisture is absorbed—about 30 minutes. Season to taste with salt, pepper. Add all remaining ingredients and mix lightly. Turn into casserole and keep warm in low oven until ready to serve. Serves 4.
Serve with: game birds and small game stews.

Savory Wild Rice with Raisins

1½ cups wild rice
½ cup minced onion
1 tablespoon butter or margarine
3 cups beef bouillon
¾ cup seedless raisins or dried currants, soaked in boiling water until plump

Wash and thoroughly drain rice, discarding any stems or floating hulls. Sauté onion in butter until transparent. Add rice and bouillon. Cook, covered, over low heat until rice is tender and bouillon has been completely absorbed (about 35 minutes). Drain raisins and add to the hot rice. Serves 6.
Goes with: all wild game.

Mushrooms and Wild Rice

¾ pound fresh mushrooms, sliced thick
    Dash lemon juice
½ stick butter or margarine
    Salt, pepper
 1 cup sour cream
¼ teaspoon nutmeg
 3 cups hot, cooked wild rice

Sprinkle mushrooms with lemon juice and sauté in butter until just tender (do not brown). Season with salt, pepper. Stir in sour cream. Add nutmeg. Serve in ring of wild rice. Serves 6.

Serve with: pheasant, duck, other game birds.

Rice Pilaf

1 cup long-grain white rice
1 tablespoon butter or margarine
4 big green onions, tops included, chopped
1 cup drained, canned plum tomatoes, chopped
1 can (10½-ounce) chicken or beef consommé, undiluted
    Salt, pepper

Sauté onions in melted butter for about 3 minutes in a flameproof casserole. Add tomatoes, rice, and consommé and bring to boil. Remove from heat, add salt and pepper to taste, and place in preheated 350° F. oven for 20 minutes or until rice is cooked. Serves 4.

Serve with: broiled small game and game birds.

Fried Hominy

1 can or 3½ cups of cooked hominy
1 egg, lightly beaten
½ teaspoon salt
¼ teaspoon pepper
½ teaspoon grated onion
2 tablespoons flour
½ stick butter or margarine, or more as needed

Drain hominy and mix with all ingredients except butter. Shape into 6–8 round, flat patties and fry in butter until golden and crisp. Serves 4–6.

Serve with: rabbit, squirrel, woodchuck, opossum, rail, duck, and other game birds.

Note: Patties may be shaped in squares and cut in triangles.

Butter-Crumb Noodles

3 cups wide noodles
3 quarts Game Bird Stock (page 190) or water with 3 table-spoons salt added
½ cup coarse dry bread crumbs
¾ stick butter or margarine
2 tablespoons poppy seeds (optional)

Bring stock or water to boil and add noodles slowly, keeping water boiling. Continue to boil for 9–10 minutes or until just tender but not soft. Stir occasionally to prevent sticking. Drain thoroughly in colander. If cooked in water, rinse with boiling water poured over. Keep hot over pan of boiling water. Sauté crumbs in butter until lightly browned and stir in poppy seeds, if desired. Pour over noodles to serve. Serves 6 or more.

Serve with: all varieties of game.

Note: Green spinach noodles are an attractive variation.

Spaetzle

3 cups flour, sifted
2 eggs
1 cup cold water
  Pinch nutmeg

Make a well in the flour and drop in the eggs. Mix, add cold water, and beat till smooth. Chill in refrigerator for 3–4 hours. When ready to cook, bring a large pot of salted water to boil and when rapidly boiling, drop the dough in this way: Put dough on plate, slant it over the boiling water, and as it rolls over the edge, quickly cut batter into tiny (1- x ¼-inch) pieces, dropping them into the water. Use a spoon or knife. Cover pot and boil till tender (about 8–9 minutes). Serves 4–6.
Serve with: game dishes that have rich gravy to pour over the spaetzle; or serve hot, buttered and parslied.

Chestnut Purée

2 pounds chestnuts
½ teaspoon salt
¼ teaspoon freshly ground white pepper
1 teaspoon sugar
1 tablespoon sweet butter, melted
1 tablespoon cream, slightly heated

With a sharp knife, split chestnut shells at pointed ends. Put chestnuts in a saucepan with water to cover and boil until shells peel off easily (about 30 minutes). Or place them on a baking sheet under the broiler for 5 minutes or until they peel easily. Put the peeled chestnuts in boiling water with the salt and simmer until tender. Rub off skins. Return to boiling water and cook till soft. Drain thoroughly. Mash or put through food mill. Season with the pepper and sugar. Stir in the melted butter and cream. Correct seasoning to taste. Makes about 2 cups.
Use with: venison dishes.
Note: To reheat, put the purée in a saucepan with a little more melted butter or cream and stir well.

Parsley Potato Dumplings

6 medium potatoes, peeled and coarsely grated
4 slices white bread, crusts trimmed
1 cup cold water or milk
½ teaspoon salt
1 medium onion, peeled and coarsely grated
2 tablespoons fresh parsley, minced fine
2 eggs beaten till frothy
¼ cup all-purpose flour
2 quarts boiling, salted water

Press grated potatoes between paper towels to remove as much water as possible. Soak bread in water for a minute or two; squeeze out water and mix bread with the salt, onion, parsley, potato, and eggs. Shape into balls about 1½ inches in diameter and roll each in flour. Lower balls into the boiling water, cover, and boil for 12 minutes. Serves 6.
Serve with: any game stew, ragout, or pot roast.

Whipped Potatoes and Turnips

1 pound turnips, peeled, sliced thin
1 pound potatoes, peeled, sliced thin
½ teaspoon sugar
    Pinch nutmeg
½ stick butter or margarine
½ teaspoon salt
¼ teaspoon pepper
2 tablespoons light cream or milk
1 tablespoons minced fresh parsley

Cover turnips and potatoes with water, add sugar, and boil for 15–20 minutes or until tender. Drain thoroughly, pressing excess moisture out with wooden spoon. Add all remaining ingredients except parsley and mash and whip with a large fork or a small electric beater. Turn into heated serving bowl and sprinkle with parsley. Serves 4–6.
Serve with: all forms of game.

Baked Apples

8 or more firm baking apples, washed
  Currant jelly
2 teaspoons butter or margarine
1 cup water
1 tablespoon lemon juice

Core each apple without breaking or piercing the blossom end. Fill each with currant jelly and top with about ¼ teaspoon butter. Place on baking sheet with at least 1-inch rim all around. Pour in water and lemon juice and bake at 400° F. for 40 minutes or until tender. Serves 8.

Serve with: goose, duck, peccary, hare.

Note: Centers of apples may be filled with sugar and a pinch of cinnamon or nutmeg instead of the jelly.

Spiced Crab Apples

4 pounds whole, perfect crab apples
6 cups cider vinegar
8 cups brown sugar, tightly packed
4 teaspoons red cinnamon candies
2 teaspoons whole cloves
1 small piece (2 inches) stick cinnamon

Wash apples, leaving stems on. Put all remaining ingredients in a large kettle and bring to boil, stirring until sugar is dissolved. Add the apples and boil until tender but still firm and full-skinned. Fill sterilized canning jars with the hot apples and pour syrup over them. Seal at once. Makes about 2 quarts.

Serve with: goose, turkey, pheasant, boar, peccary.

Note: Recipe may be used for equivalent amount of small Seckel pears which should first be pared, then sprinkled with lemon juice.

Onions Curaçao

24 small whole onions, peeled
1 teaspoon salt
½ stick butter or margarine
3 tablespoons curaçao

Cover onions with water, add salt, and boil for 8–10 minutes. Drain thoroughly. Melt butter in skillet and add onions, turning constantly and sautéeing until golden brown. Add the curaçao, stir through, and serve at once. Serves 4.
Serve with: pheasant, turkey, rabbit.

Rosemary Onions

1 dozen medium to small yellow onions of uniform size, peeled
1 tablespoon sugar
1 teaspoon salt
1 teaspoon dried rosemary or 2 teaspoons of fresh
1 tablespoon butter or margarine

Cover onions with water and boil till tender but still crisp —about 20 minutes. Add the sugar, salt, and rosemary when water comes to boil. Drain. Melt butter and gently heat onions through, turning to coat all surfaces with the butter. Serves 4–6.
Serve with: game birds and big game roasts, chops and steaks.

Fennel in Cream

4 large heads of fennel (or finocchi)

½ stick butter or margarine

1 medium onion, chopped fine

½ pint cream

   Salt, pepper

1 tablespoon instant flour

2 tablespoons bread crumbs, lightly browned in butter

Trim any bruised leaves from the fennel and cut off the tops. Cut each head in quarters, then each quarter in half. Cover with water in a saucepan and boil until tender but still crisp—about 12–15 minutes. Drain and place in heat-proof casserole. Meanwhile, sauté onion in the butter until transparent. Pour onion and butter over the fennel. Add cream and salt and pepper to taste. Sprinkle and swirl in the instant flour. Top with the bread crumbs and place in a 350° F. oven for 15 minutes. Serves 4–6.

Serve with: goose, duck, pheasant, and other game birds.

Brussels Sprouts with Chestnuts

1 quart fresh Brussels sprouts, trimmed, washed

½ teaspoon salt

20 cooked, peeled chestnuts

½ stick butter or margarine

Boil sprouts in water to cover with the salt for about 10 minutes or until tender, but still crisp. Drain. Melt butter in saucepan and toss sprouts and chestnuts in it till thoroughly coated and heated through. Serves 4–6.

Brussels Sprouts with Grapes

1 quart baby Brussels sprouts
½ teaspoon salt
2 tablespoons butter
1½ cups seedless green grapes
1 teaspoon coriander seed

Wash and trim sprouts and boil in water to cover for 10–15 minutes or until tender but crunchy. Drain and sprinkle with salt. Melt butter in saucepan and toss grapes and coriander seed in it over medium heat for 3–4 minutes. Add sprouts and lightly mix grapes and sprouts. Heat through. Serves 4.

Sauerkraut in Wine

1 quart sauerkraut
1 pint white wine
1 large potato, peeled, grated
1 large tart apple, peeled, cored, diced
   Salt, pepper

Simmer sauerkraut, wine, potato, and apple for 1½–2 hours and season with salt, pepper to taste. Serves 6–8.
Use with: duck, goose, pheasant.
Note: For smaller amount, halve the sauerkraut and wine and continue preparation. Serves 3–4.

Braised Celery

12 long, tender stalks celery, washed and trimmed
1½ cups good beef bouillon
¼ teaspoon celery seed
2 tablespoons butter or margarine
1 tablespoon flour
¼ teaspoon salt
Freshly ground white pepper
Paprika

Cut celery stalks in thirds. Simmer in the bouillon with celery seed until tender but still crisp. Remove celery and reserve the bouillon. Melt butter in a skillet, stir in flour, and cook over medium heat until golden brown. Slowly stir in the heated bouillon and bring to a boil, stirring until slightly thickened. Add the celery, and salt and pepper to taste. Serve with paprika sprinkled over. Serves 4–6.
Serve with: game birds, venison, and big game roasts.

Braised Endive

6 medium stalks endive
2 cups boiling water
1 teaspoon lemon juice
2 slices bacon, diced
1 small onion, thinly sliced
1½ tablespoons butter or margarine
1 cup chicken stock or bouillon
½ teaspoon salt
Pinch white pepper
1 tablespoon cornstarch mixed with 2 tablespoons cold water

Clean the endive stalks and split them lengthwise. Pour boiling water and lemon juice over them and let stand for about 5 minutes. Drain thoroughly. In a large skillet over medium heat put the bacon, onion, and butter. When butter is melted, lay the endive halves side by side on top and pour the stock over. Sprinkle with salt, pepper. Cover tightly, lower heat, and simmer gently for about 30 minutes or until endive is tender. Add the cornstarch mixed with water, turn up heat, and stir pan juices around endive until slightly thickened. Add additional salt, pepper to taste. Serves 4.
Serve with: all game; especially with pheasant, turkey, quail, dove, pigeon, grouse.

Spicy White Cabbage

1 firm young head white cabbage (about 1 pound)
3 tablespoons vegetable oil
3 tablespoons white vinegar
2 tablespoons sugar
3 whole cloves
2 large cooking apples, peeled, cored, sliced
½ teaspoon salt
2 tablespoons curaçao or Triple Sec

Cut up cabbage in coarse shred or thin slices. Heat oil in large, deep skillet or Dutch oven. Add cabbage and stir to coat thoroughly with oil. Add all remaining ingredients, stir through, and simmer, tightly covered, for 1 hour over low heat. Serves 4.

Serve with: duck, rabbit, goose, venison.

Bavarian Cabbage

1 large head (about 3½ pounds) red cabbage, coarsely shredded
¼ cup vegetable oil
2 firm red apples, cored, sliced
1 medium onion, sliced thin
1 teaspoon salt
1 tablespoon vinegar
1 tablespoon sugar
¼ teaspoon powdered cloves
½ cup red wine
½ cup water

Heat oil in a large cast-iron skillet (with cover) or a heavy, heatproof casserole. Sauté onion until transparent. Add all remaining ingredients, cover, and simmer for about 2 hours or until tender and limp. Stir occasionally and add more water if cabbage becomes too dry. Serves 6–8.

Serve with: duck, goose, roast venison and game pot roasts.

Baked Acorn Squash

4 medium acorn squash
8 teaspoons brown sugar
4 slices bacon
  Powdered ginger
  Powdered cinnamon

Wash, cut in half lengthwise, and seed the squash. Arrange the halves close together on a large baking sheet. In each half put a teaspoon of brown sugar, a pinch of ginger, and a pinch of cinnamon. Top with a half slice of bacon. Bake at 350° F. for 30 minutes or until tender. Serves 8.
Serve with: roast venison, elk, moose, boar, or large game birds.
Note: Recipe may be halved, quartered for fewer servings.

Pecan-Rice Orange Cups

2 cups chicken stock or broth
1 cup uncooked rice
2 tablespoons butter or margarine
2/3 cup coarsely chopped pecans
2 tablespoons minced parsley
1/4 teaspoon salt
1/8 teaspoon powdered nutmeg
6 orange shells (scooped out halves of 3 oranges)

Combine chicken stock and rice in a saucepan and bring to boil. Stir through and cover, cooking over low heat for 10–14 minutes or until rice is still firm but tender. Stir in butter, pecans, parsley, salt, and nutmeg. Fill orange shells with the mixture and arrange around serving platter of duck, pheasant, turkey, or other game birds. Serves 6.
Note: Orange shells may be scalloped or saw-toothed around edges if desired.

Baked Stuffed Mushrooms

12 large white mushrooms
¼ stick butter or margarine
 1 large stalk celery, top included, chopped fine
 1 medium onion, chopped fine
½ teaspoons dried oregano
 2 tablespoons fine, dry bread crumbs
 2 tablespoons milk or 1 whole egg, lightly beaten
   Salt, pepper
   Butter or margarine

Remove mushroom stems. Melt butter in a skillet, chop and sauté the stems, celery, and onion along with the oregano. Add the bread crumbs, milk, and salt and pepper to taste. Fill mushroom caps and place on baking sheet. Dot with butter and sprinkle with additional salt, pepper. Bake at 400° F. for 15 minutes. Serves 4.
Serve with: roasts, birds, chops, cutlets.

Braised Escarole Amandine

 1 head (about 1 pound) escarole, trimmed, washed, drained
 1 tablespoon butter or margarine
½ teaspoon salt
¾ cup chicken stock, broth, or bouillon
¼ fresh lime
 2 tablespoons slivered, blanched almonds

Melt butter in large saucepan. Put whole head of escarole in pan and add salt and chicken stock. Cover tightly. Bring to boil, lower heat, and simmer for 25–30 minutes. Serve hot with juice of the lime and almonds sprinkled over. Serves 4–6.

Stewed Apples

4 large, firm apples, cored, sliced ¼ inch thick
1½ tablespoons butter or margarine
1 large onion, sliced thin
½ teaspoon salt
3 tablespoons sugar
½ teaspoon lemon juice

Melt butter in skillet and sauté apples and onion slices, sprinkle with sugar and lemon juice, and cover tightly. Simmer over low heat for 10–15 minutes or until apples are tender. Serves 4.
Serve with: goose, duck, game stews.

Whole Fresh Cranberry Sauce

1 quart cranberries, washed, cleaned
1 cup sugar
1 cup water
¼ teaspoon powdered cloves
½ teaspoon cinnamon
⅛ teaspoon nutmeg
1 tablespoon lemon juice

Put all ingredients into a large kettle, bring to boil, lower heat, and simmer for 10–15 minutes or until berries pop. Remove berries with skimmer and continue cooking juice over low heat till it is the consistency of thick syrup. Pour over berries. Makes about 2½ cups.
Serve with: turkey, pheasant, goose, duck.

Wild Beach Plum Jelly

4 cups wild beach plum juice (about 4½ pounds plums plus
    ½ cup water)
7½ cups sugar
½ bottle liquid pectin

Place sorted and washed plums in large kettle. Crush fruit, add water, cover and bring to boil. Lower heat and simmer for 10–15 minutes. Strain juice in a jelly bag or fruit press. (The clearest jelly comes from juice that has dripped through a jelly bag without pressing, but a greater amount of juice can be obtained by twisting bag tightly and squeezing it.) Measure juice into clean kettle. Stir in sugar. Place on high heat and, stirring constantly, bring quickly to a full, rolling boil that cannot be stirred down. Add pectin, bring again to full rolling boil, and boil hard for 1 minute. Remove from heat; skim foam. Pour immediately into hot, sterilized jars and seal with ⅛ inch of hot paraffin. Makes about 11 6-ounce glasses.

Serve with: duck, goose, venison.

Use for: sauces calling for tart jelly.

Cranberry Relish

4 cups fresh cranberries, washed, picked over
1 large navel orange, quartered, seeded, peel on
1 teaspoon fresh lemon juice
1 tablespoon grated or shredded lemon rind
⅛ teaspoon powdered cloves
2 cups granulated sugar

Put all ingredients except cloves and sugar through a food grinder with medium disc or blade. Add the sugar and cloves and mix well. Refrigerate in covered bowl or jars overnight. Makes about 5 cups.

Serve with: turkey, pheasant, and other game birds, as well as with game meats.

Note: Relish may be kept, covered, in refrigerator for several weeks, and it improves with age.

Prune-Raisin Relish

1 cup raisins
1 cup pitted prunes, coarsely chopped
1 medium onion, chopped fine
1 teaspoon chili powder
1 bottle (12-ounce) chili sauce
2 tablespoons lemon juice
1 cup water

Mix together the raisins, chopped prunes, onion, and chili powder. Combine chili sauce, lemon juice, and water in a saucepan and bring to a boil over medium heat. Pour over raisin-prune mixture. Cool and refrigerate for 2 or more hours. Makes about 3½ cups.
Serve with: bear steak or roast.

Potato Stuffing

3 cups hot mashed potatoes
1½ cups coarse dry bread crumbs
1 large onion, chopped fine, sautéed in butter
1 teaspoon salt
1 teaspoon powdered sage
3 tablespoons minced fresh parsley
½ teaspoon celery salt
¼ teaspoon marjoram
2 lightly beaten eggs

Mix together all ingredients. Let cool and fill cavity. Makes enough for a 10–12 pound bird.
Use for: goose, turkey.

Chestnut Stuffing

3 tablespoons butter or margarine
2 tablespoons coarsely chopped onion
1 turkey, goose, or chicken liver, chopped fine
½ teaspoon salt
¼ teaspoon pepper
1 pound fresh sausage meat, fried golden-brown
¼ teaspoon poultry seasoning
¼ cup sherry or port
1 egg, lightly beaten
30 cooked and crumbled chestnuts
1 teaspoon chopped parsley
¼ teaspoon dried sage

Melt butter and cook onion until limp and translucent. Remove from heat and stir in the chopped liver; add salt, pepper. Turn into a bowl and add and mix in order all remaining ingredients. Makes enough for a medium-size goose, small turkey, or two small pheasants.

Olive Wild Rice Stuffing

2 cups cooked wild rice or 1 cup of brown rice and 1 cup of wild rice
1¼ cups pitted, chopped ripe or green olives
2 teaspoons instant minced onion flakes
1 stick butter or margarine, melted
½ teaspoon salt
  Pinch pepper
  Pinch oregano
1 tablespoon minced fresh parsley

Combine all ingredients, mixing together lightly with a fork. Makes enough for a 4- to 5-pound bird.

Sausage Stuffing

1 large onion, coarsely chopped
1 stick of butter or margarine
1 pound of sausage meat, lightly fried
1 goose or turkey liver, chopped, sautéed in butter
  Juice and grated rind of 1 lemon
2 eggs, lightly beaten
1 tablespoon chopped fresh parsley
½ cup dry bread crumbs
½ teaspoon thyme
½ teaspoon sage
½ teaspoon salt
¼ teaspoon freshly ground black pepper

Sauté the onion in butter until soft. Combine with all remaining ingredients. Makes enough for 1 small goose or turkey.

Small Bird Stuffing

½ stick butter or margarine
2 game bird livers, chopped
1 small onion, chopped fine
3 medium mushrooms, chopped fine
2 slices cold boiled ham, chopped fine
1½ cups coarse bread crumbs
½ teaspoon salt
  Pinch white pepper
¼ teaspoon marjoram
  Pinch thyme
  Pinch sage
½ teaspoon dried parsley
1 egg, lightly beaten

Melt butter over medium heat and sauté livers, onion, mushrooms, and ham until golden brown. Add bread crumbs and seasonings and stir for a minute or two. Remove from heat and allow to cool for 5–10 minutes. Lightly and thoroughly mix in the egg. Makes enough for 4 small partridges or 2 grouse.

Brown Rice Stuffing

1 pound chicken livers
2 medium onions, chopped fine
1 large green pepper, seeded, chopped fine
1 large clove garlic, minced
1 stick butter or margarine
1/2 teaspoon thyme
2 tablespoons chopped fresh parsley
1/2 teaspoon salt
1/4 teaspoon pepper
2 1/2 cups cooked brown or white rice

Melt butter in large skillet and sauté chicken livers, onion, green pepper, and garlic until tender, but not brown. Break up livers with fork in small pieces. Remove from heat. Add and stir gently together all remaining ingredients. Makes enough for 8 small birds, a large goose, or large turkey.

Prune-Apple Dressing

2 dozen large pitted prunes, chopped
  White wine or orange juice
6 firm cooking apples, peeled, cored, diced
1 teaspoon instant minced onion
1/4 teaspoon powdered cloves

Soak chopped prunes in wine or juice to cover overnight. Mix all ingredients together and fill cavity of bird loosely. Makes enough for a 10- to 12-pound bird.
Use for: stuffing goose, turkey, or pheasants.
Note: Prunes may be left whole and apples thinly sliced, if desired.

Sage and Onion Dressing

1 pound yellow onions, peeled, chopped fine
1 quart boiling water
1 teaspoon salt
2 cups dry, coarse bread crumbs
½ teaspoon salt
¼ teaspoon freshly ground black pepper
2 teaspoons crumbled dried sage
   Pinch paprika
½ stick melted butter
1 egg, beaten lightly

Place onions in a large sieve and pour over them the boiling water to which the salt has been added. Let drain and mix them with all remaining ingredients, tossing lightly with a fork. Makes enough for a 6- to 7-pound bird.
Use for: duck, small goose, turkey.

Big Game Stock

2–3 pounds deer, elk, or moose bones, cracked or sawed into
        2- to 3-inch pieces, preferably with meat clinging to them
   2 large carrots, cut in thick rounds
   3 medium onions, quartered
3–4 sprigs parsley
   6 crushed peppercorns
   1 clove garlic, crushed
   1 bay leaf
      Pinch nutmeg
   2 stalks celery, tops included, chopped
   1 large turnip, peeled, quartered
  ½ teaspoon thyme

In a large, deep kettle, cover bones with water and add all remaining ingredients. Bring to boil, lower heat, skim any scum from surface, and simmer for about 3 hours or until all meat falls from bones. Cool. Remove fat from top. Strain and refrigerate.
Note: For a richer stock, brown the bones with meat attached in a few tablespoons of hot oil before adding water.

Game Bird Stock

1 or more game bird carcasses and bones
3 sprigs parsley per carcass
2 celery stalk tops per carcass
1 teaspoon salt
¼ teaspoon pepper

Cut up the carcass and crush or crack the bones. Put all in a kettle, cover with water, and place over low heat. Simmer, covered, for 2 hours or more. Add remaining ingredients and simmer for 30 minutes more. Cool and skim fat from surface. Strain and keep refrigerated for use in preparing game birds.

Note: Use quail, pheasant, ruffed (not sage or pinnated) grouse, pigeon, or dove carcasses. Quail, pheasant, and grouse carcasses combine well together, and pigeon and dove work well together. So-called "gamey" birds—sage and pinnated grouse, ducks and shorebirds—need the addition of more seasonings: a clove of garlic, an onion, a pinch of nutmeg, and several sprigs of thyme, marjoram, and parsley.

Since a feast of game for most people is not an everyday affair, the bird or beast at table deserves its bottle—as does the cook or host or hostess who serves it forth. The choice of that spirited accompaniment, of course, is highly subjective and a matter of personal taste buds. Rules of "red wine with red meat and white with white" have long ago been amicably broken, and in today's era of wining and dining the strict conformist is rare. Both the cook and the sommelier in the home are urged to experiment and be creative. However, for those who have neither preconceived ideas nor special preferences and who wish to know "what goes with what," here are some elementary guidelines.

In general, a dry red wine of good vintage is the best accompaniment for all wild game. If white wine has been used in the preparation of a dish, then a fine, dry white wine may well be indicated; better yet, if the dinner is exceptionally elegant with, say, a superbly served pheasant in cream, then champagne is eminently appropriate. At the other end of this gastronomic scale are the succulent, often robust, peasant dishes—ragouts and stews of squirrel, muskrat, raccoon, and opossum—and these may be more happily complemented by a good lager, an ale, or a bock beer when in season. If a national or ethnic specialty is on the menu, such as German-style wild goose, then the *vin du pays* is a good selection—in this case, one of the German white wines most traditionally served in that country.

Always consider the sauce and the nature of the ingredients used in the preparation of game. Taste is the determining factor. A light-fleshed bird served in a subtle cream sauce is even more delectable when complemented by a fine, dry white wine. But if the bird or beast at table is cooked in a highly flavored sauce and its flesh is rich and gamey, then the wine should match these tastes with richness, body, taste, and intensity. More delicate dishes are best balanced with the lighter wines—either white or red. A highly spiced, hot and peppery dish—akin to Indonesian, Mexican, and certain Creole cookery—is more favorably offset by an accompanying beer or ale to quell the inner fires. Dishes with a highly acid content, such as birds stuffed or cooked with sauerkraut, also invite beer; serving wine with these could be an injustice to a good vintage, a conflict of tastes rather than a complement.

Consider, too, the temperature, both of the weather and the dish. Cold game dishes—the pâtés, terrines, et al.—are beautifully enhanced in hot weather by cool, light white wines as well as the rosés.

Overall, the big reds are in perfect taste and harmony with all big game dishes—the roasts, chops, and steaks of venison, moose, caribou, antelope, elk, and the like (a few exceptions are noted later).

At the top of the list would be a well-aged Bordeaux—Médoc, St. Emilion, Pomerol—or a great vintage California Cabernet. Equally satisfying would be a Côtes du Rhône—Hermitage, Châteauneuf-du-Pape—or one of the robust Burgundies— from Côte de Beaune, Côte de Nuits, et al. Then there are the full-flavored, rich red Cabernet wines from Hungary, Yugoslavia, and Chile, or some of the finer Chiantis and Barolos from Italy, as well as the Spanish Rioja and the California Barbera or Petite Sirah, all of which, well-aged, serve pleasantly.

With wild boar and the collared peccary, the red wines are acceptable because of the richness of the meat. However, some of the dry whites suggested later for drinking with some of the white-fleshed birds are also suitable.

Beer aficionados recommend a good dark beer with hare, especially hasenpfeffer, and with venison pot roasts or other dark-meat big game braised roasts. Imported German and Danish beers are high on the list. The rugged, nearly black stout, some of the ales, and now and then a tankard of porter go well with hunters' game stews—especially in the field at the campsite. The seasonal bock beer, as noted, is another fine complement to the foregoing dishes.

As for the birds at the feast, the choice is legion. With ducks of all species, consider, as well as the foregoing reds, a Beaujolais, a fine claret, or a Pinot Noir. Salute the turkey or goose in style with a robust Burgundy; or complement the goose in the German tradition with a Moselle or Rhine wine on occasion.

As stated, champagne is always a festive note with pheasant and a perfect complement. But a white Burgundy or one of the great Alsatian whites is also fitting for this delectable bird. Quail, too, suggests champagne with any haute cuisine presentation, or a Rhine, Moselle, or white Burgundy. The same applies for partridge, grouse, and similar birds. With snipe, a good bet is a Médoc—a Lascombes, Margaux, or Beychevelle; and with doves, a white Burgundy—a Montrachet or a Meursault.

Wine fanciers among the guests may be sensitive about the serving of an excellent, rare bottle with a dish that contains tart jelly and fruit sauces of a sharp nature—a sacrilege in most eyes. If such is the case and the recipe demands these ingredients to accent the game, then the menu dilemma may be solved by serving a lesser wine or a fine ale or imported beer.

If dry white wines are indeed preferred with white-meated birds, with cold birds and game pâtés, good choices include: a dry Graves, a Chassagne-Montrachet, or Meursault (as noted); a Macon Blanc, a Pouilly-Fuissé, a Chablis, a California Sauvignon Blanc or Traminer. The whites need not always be dry. As a matter of fact the fruitier German and Alsatian wines often add a pleasant note to the flavors of wild game birds. And if mellower whites are preferred—somewhere between dry and sweet and, in fact, semisweet—then the choice might be a Rhine (domestic or imported), a Moselle, a Vouvray, or a Chenin Blanc.

Above all, the accompanying beverage should never overpower, never upstage the dish. It should balance, underscore, and complement it, bringing out those savory wild flavor tastes and the delicious nuances of the attendant sauces and gravies.

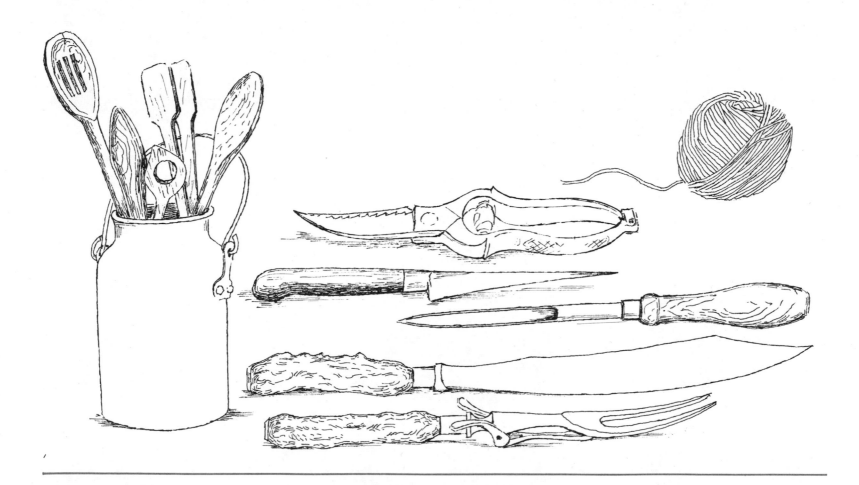

Most of the smaller birds may be very simply trussed by tying the legs with butcher's cord or string close to the body. The cord is tied around the end of one drumstick, carried across the secured and filled cavity, and drawn and tied tightly around the other drumstick. Wings may be turned back and under the bird.

Larger birds such as pheasant may be trussed with one continuous piece of cord, as shown in the sketches.

Very small birds such as doves and quail may be quickly and easily trussed as shown.

1. With bird breast side up, lay cord across drumstick ends.

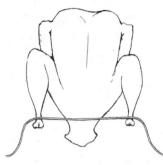

2. Bring cord ends around drumstick ends and up, crossing the two ends over the closed cavity.

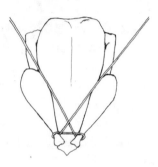

3. Draw cord ends tight, pulling drumstick ends together, and carrying ends of cord up over legs.

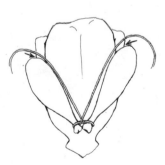

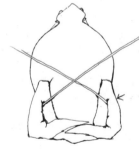

4. Turn bird over and pull cord ends through second joints of folded-back wings.

5. Bring cord ends together, drawing them tight, and tie snugly and securely; snip off ends.

For very small birds, insert boning knife point near end of one drumstick and make a 1-inch slit through the leg, between tendon and bone. Insert drumstick end of other leg through slit.

Game meat unless pen-raised tends to be very lean, and larding or barding it prevents dryness and adds juiciness. This is most often done with fat salt pork or fatty bacon. To lard a fillet or game roast, "lardoons" must be prepared. These are strips of fat salt pork or fatty bacon cut into 2-inch (or longer, if desired) strips, ¼ inch wide and ¼ inch thick. Chill the fat to facilitate cutting. (Recipes throughout the recipe section specify amounts needed.) Use a larding needle as shown in number 2, and, after making a slit in the surface of the meat, insert the lardoons at 1- or 2-inch intervals, always across the grain. Lardoons may be seasoned as desired, and strips of ham for flavor may also be used as lardoons.

To lard a bird, insert lardoons in breast at right angles to the breastbone.

Barding is simply covering a bird with strips of fatty bacon or fat salt pork. These strips should be about ¼ inch thick and sufficiently large to cover the breast and legs, or, in the case of a small bird, to wrap completely around bird.

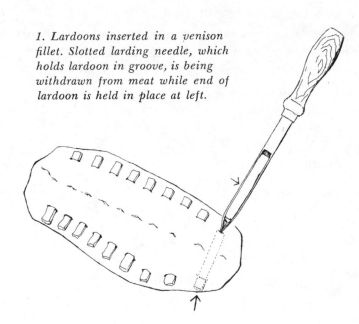

1. Lardoons inserted in a venison fillet. Slotted larding needle, which holds lardoon in groove, is being withdrawn from meat while end of lardoon is held in place at left.

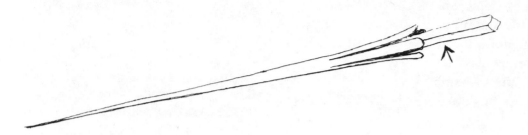

2. *Another type of larding needle.*
Lardoon is inserted in flared end
which is flexible and may be spread
to insert lardoon, then pinched
together to hold it.

3. *Barded game bird with salt*
pork strips slit in centers
and draped over breast. When
wrapping bird completely,
cord may be used to tie
barding in place.

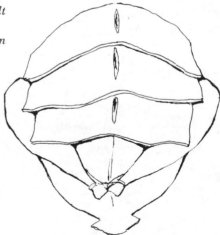

The right tools and sharp tools, as for any carving, are essential to carving game for the table. Basically and minimally, four items are necessary: a carving knife, fork, slicer, and poultry shears. The kitchen boning knife may also be helpful in some instances. Illustrated here are the basics of carving or cutting up game birds when they are presented whole at the table.

TURKEY

1. Begin with legs to carver's right. Work on one side of bird at a time, cutting off thigh with leg attached by carving down between thigh and body. Steady bird with fork.

3. Transfer leg and thigh to serving platter and cut thigh from leg by severing at joint.

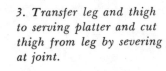

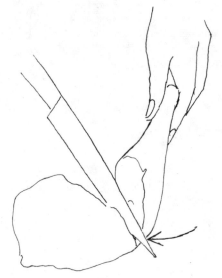

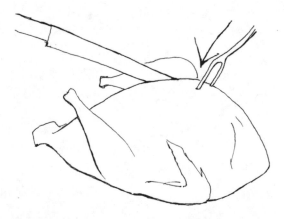

2. Insert fork in leg and pull thigh and leg away from body, cutting down between joint and severing from body.

4. Slice thigh meat and, if drumstick is not to be served whole, hold it vertically and slice down.

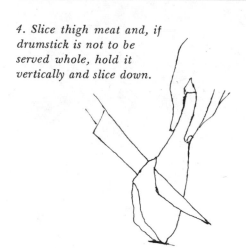

5. Using fork, press wing away and down from body and slice at joint to sever.

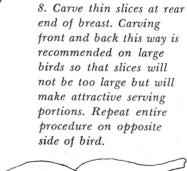

8. Carve thin slices at rear end of breast. Carving front and back this way is recommended on large birds so that slices will not be too large but will make attractive serving portions. Repeat entire procedure on opposite side of bird.

7. Carve breast in thin slices beginning halfway up on front of breast until bone is touched.

6. Cut horizontally at base of breast, so that meat, when sliced, will fall away neatly.

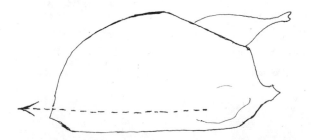

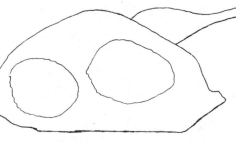

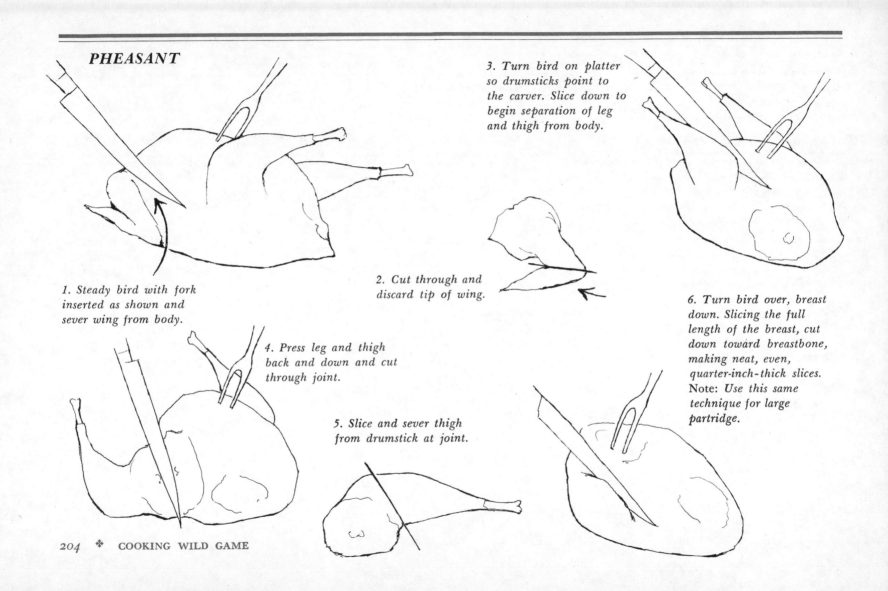

PHEASANT

1. Steady bird with fork inserted as shown and sever wing from body.

2. Cut through and discard tip of wing.

3. Turn bird on platter so drumsticks point to the carver. Slice down to begin separation of leg and thigh from body.

4. Press leg and thigh back and down and cut through joint.

5. Slice and sever thigh from drumstick at joint.

6. Turn bird over, breast down. Slicing the full length of the breast, cut down toward breastbone, making neat, even, quarter-inch-thick slices. Note: *Use this same technique for large partridge.*

GOOSE

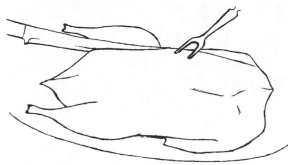

1. Insert fork as shown . and tilt bird on an angle. Holding bird firmly with fork, slice around leg to loosen it.

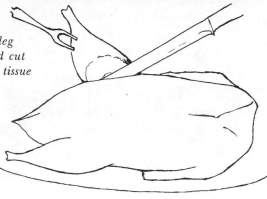

2. With fork, pull leg away from body and cut through connective tissue at joint. Sever leg.

3. Slice leg neatly in thin slices parallel to the bone.

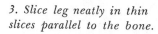

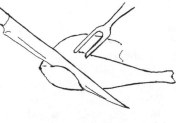

4. Cutting straight across the bird, remove neck end.

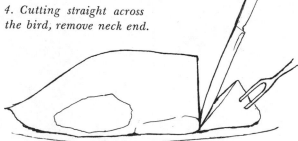

5. With slicing knife, cut even, thin slices the entire length of the bird, parallel to the breastbone.

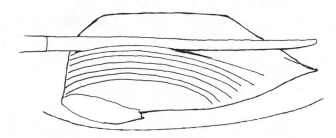

DUCK

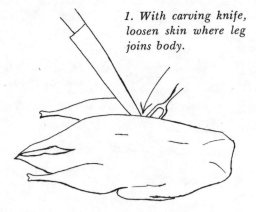

1. With carving knife, loosen skin where leg joins body.

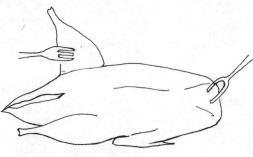

2. Insert carving fork in neck or, if not stuffed, in body cavity to steady bird. With another fork, pull leg away from body.

3. Sever leg and thigh by carving through joint. Then cut thigh from leg, if desired, or leave whole.

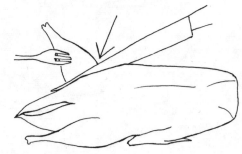

4. Halve the breast meat by slicing close to breast-bone with a to-the-bone cut from tail to neck.

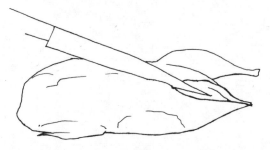

5. Holding bird with carving fork, use second fork and pull off half the breast with wing in one piece. Alternate way: Slice breast meat in thin slices from neck to tail parallel to breastbone. Remove wings last.

6. *Small ducks (tern, and others) may be served simply by halving the birds horizontally with poultry shears.*

7. *Another way to serve small ducks: Halve them by carving straight across the middle as sketched.*

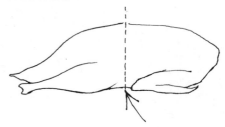

Quail and other small birds such as snipe and dove may be served whole or split as shown in the sketches.

QUAIL

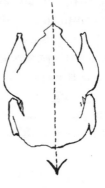

1. Place bird breast down and cut through from tail to neck.

2. Serve, skin side up, in halves as sketched.

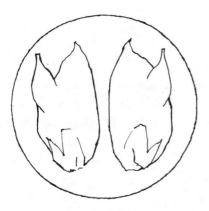

Because deer, elk, antelope, and other big game are butchered into cuts similar to beef and veal, the basic carving techniques for the latter generally apply to game meat. Roasts of all kinds (as well as very large game birds) are more easily carved if they are allowed to stand for about 15 minutes before cutting. Rare meat, depending on the size of the roast, will need a longer "rest" period—up to half an hour. Keep the meat warm in a tent of aluminum foil. Cutlets and steaks, of course, are carved and served at once.

The rule of cutting across the grain of meat applies in all carving where practical and feasible. And thicker slices are always juicer than thin ones. Keep the carving fork just behind the knife when carving and aim for even, uniform slices. Pierce the meat with the fork as little as possible in order to conserve precious juices.

A *leg of venison* is traditionally sliced toward the carver —much like carving a leg of lamb which differs only in that the latter is sliced away from the carver.

A *rack of venison* is carved with the tips of the bones pointing toward the carver and the ribs exposed so that the carver may easily see where to cut between ribs.

A *fillet* is carved the whole length in thin slices with the carving knife slightly angled.

A *saddle of venison* is the most complicated to carve. First, detach the two sides of the top part of the saddle by cutting the whole length with a very long knife. The exposed fillet should next be cut across in thin slices, the whole length. Replace the slices without cutting the sides which are rolled underneath when presented for serving. The legs are carved individually as previously noted.

Following are lists of where to buy: 1) game, 2) special ingredients for cooking game (spices, herbs, and seasonings), and 3) kitchen equipment and utensils for preparing game. In each group the stores are listed by cities. Those starred (*) will handle mail orders, but query first. *Note:* Lists are by no means complete; many fine markets and stores have been omitted for lack of space.

Game Markets

Laws govern the sale of game as well as hunting throughout the United States. Breeders who maintain private game farms and preserves are licensed. Most fine butcher shops carry pen-raised rabbit and squab, as do many well-stocked supermarkets. While not all available wild game is carried in these markets at all times, most butchers will special order with sufficient advance notice.

AUSTIN, TEXAS
Hunts Meat Market
9611 McNeil Road

BOSTON, MASSACHUSETTS
Samuel Holmes Inc.
15 Foodmart Road
South Boston

BUFFALO, NEW YORK
Zeldner's Wild Game Center
638 Clinton Street

CHICAGO, ILLINOIS
Sam Houston & Son
157 South Water Market

FRANCONIA, PENNSYLVANIA
Longacre Farms

GRAND ISLAND, NEBRASKA
*Prairie Pride Farms
Box 517   Zip 68801

LOCKPORT, ILLINOIS
Czimer Foods, Inc.
159th Street between Bell and Parker Roads
Route 7

LOS ANGELES, CALIFORNIA
Farmer's Market
Corner Fairfax Avenue and Third Street

Jurgensen's Grocery Co.
409 North Beverly Drive
Beverly Hills

MINNEAPOLIS, MINNESOTA
Crown Meat Co.

NEW YORK, NEW YORK
Iron Gate Products Co., Inc.
424 West 54 Street

Jefferson Market
455 Avenue of the Americas

Maryland Gourmet Mart, Inc.
414 Amsterdam Avenue

Ottomanelli's Meat Market
281 Bleecker Street

M. Lobel & Sons, Inc.
1096 Madison Avenue

SAN FRANCISCO, CALIFORNIA
Manley Produce
1101 Grant Avenue

WASHINGTON, D.C.
French Market
1622 Wisconsin Avenue, NW

International Safeway
1110 F Street, NW

WAYNE, PENNSLYVANIA
The Farmer's Market

Special Ingredients

While supermarkets and specialty food shops offer most of the ingredients needed for preparing the recipes in this book, some of the rarer spices and herbs are not universally available. Following are shops which carry more extensive lines. Those starred (*) will handle mail orders.

BOSTON, MASSACHUSETTS
Anthony Polcari
105 Salem Street

*Jordan Marsh
450 Washington Street   Zip 02111

CAMBRIDGE, MASSACHUSETTS
*Cambridge Coffee, Tea and Spice House
1765 Massachusetts Avenue   Zip 02140

*Cardullo's Gourmet Shop
6 Brattle Street   Zip 02138

CHICAGO, ILLINOIS
*The Epicure Shop
*Carson Pirie Scott & Co.
1 South State Street   Zip 60603

*Marshall Field & Co.
111 North State Street   Zip 60601

DALLAS, TEXAS
*The Epicure Shop
Neiman-Marcus
Main at Ervay   Zip 75201

LOS ANGELES, CALIFORNIA
*Jurgensen's Grocery Co.
409 North Beverly Drive
Beverly Hills   Zip 90210

MONTREAL, QUEBEC, CANADA
*Eaton's Gourmet Department
677 St. Catherine Street West

NEW ORLEANS, LOUISIANA
*Central Grocery
923 Decatur   Zip 70116

NEW YORK, N.Y.
*B. Altman
Fifth Avenue and 34th Street   Zip 10016

*Bloomingdale's
Lexington Avenue and 59th Street   Zip 10022

Charles Ferrari, Inc.
977 Lexington Avenue

*Lekvar by the Barrel (H. Roth & Sons)
1577 First Avenue   Zip 10028

*Paprikás Weiss Importer
1546 Second Avenue   Zip 10028

*Trinacria Importing Company
415 Third Avenue   Zip 10016

Fresh herbs are sold by the following:

Balducci Produce
424 Sixth Avenue

Charles Ferrari, Inc.
977 Lexington Avenue

Empire Fruit
1188 Madison Avenue

Jefferson Market
455 Avenue of the Americas

French Market
1622 Wisconsin Avenue, NW

International Safeway
1110 F Street, NW

Kitchen Equipment and Tools

The following stores and shops carry kitchen utensils and equipment to aid in the preparation of wild game for the table. Those starred (*) will handle mail orders, but query first about the item in which you are interested.

ATLANTA, GEORGIA
*Rich's
45 Broad Street, S.W.   Zip 30303

BOSTON, MASSACHUSETTS
*The Pot Shop
381 Boylston Street   Zip 02116

CHICAGO, ILLINOIS
*Carson Pirie Scott & Co.
1 South State Street   Zip 60603

DETROIT, MICHIGAN
*J. L. Hudson
1206 Woodward   Zip 48226

LOS ANGELES, CALIFORNIA
The May Company

NEW YORK, NEW YORK
*Bazaar de la Cuisine
160 E. 55 Street   Zip 10022

*Bazaar Français
666 6th Avenue   Zip 10010

*The Bridge Co.
212 East 52 Street   Zip 10022

*Hammacher Schlemmer
145 East 57 Street   Zip 10022

*La Cuisinière
903 Madison Avenue   Zip 10021

*Paprikás Weiss Importer
1546 Second Avenue   Zip 10028

SAN FRANCISCO, CALIFORNIA
*Williams-Sonoma
576 Sutter Street   Zip 94102

WASHINGTON, D.C.
French Kitchen
1500 Wisconsin Avenue, NW

About the Author

Zack Hanle is a third-generation game cook who spent her growing up on an island off the South Jersey coast "eating feathered, furred, finned and shelled delectables" procured by the sportsmen in her family. Author of the recent bestselling *Cooking with Flowers,* she has written more than sixty how-to handbooks and has been editor in chief of such food- and wine-oriented magazines as CBS Publications' *Epicure* and the supermarket *Everywoman's.* The collection of recipes in *Cooking Wild Game* comes from her own longtime interest in preparing and serving game, as well as from her parents' and grandparents' personal records of testing and tasting.